PHILIPPIANS

Rev. Francis R. Davis
Our Lady Of Lourdes
120 Fairmont Road
Elmira, N. Y. 14905

Scripture for Meditation: 2

PHILIPPIANS

by John Bligh

ST PAUL PUBLICATIONS

ST PAUL PUBLICATIONS,
LANGLEY, BUCKS., GREAT BRITAIN.

© 1969 ST PAUL PUBLICATIONS

NIHIL OBSTAT:
RT. REV. MGR. R. J. FOSTER, S.T.L., L.S.S.
DIE 11A NOVEMBRIS 1968.

IMPRIMATUR:
+ GEORGIUS PATRICIUS, ARCHBISHOP OF BIRMINGHAM
DIE 11A NOVEMBRIS 1968.

The "Nihil Obstat" and "Imprimatur" are a declaration that a book or pamphlet is considered to be free from doctrinal or moral error. It is not implied that those who have granted th "Nihil Obstat" and "Imprimatur" agree with the contents or statements expressed.

FIRST PUBLISHED JANUARY 1969 BY ST PAUL PUBLICATIONS AND
PRINTED IN ENGLAND BY SOCIETY OF ST PAUL, LANGLEY, BUCKS.

CONTENTS

Readiness for Judgment	9
Gratitude and Generosity	14
Kinship in Christ	19
The Suffering Servant	22
Pain and Joy	27
Detachment	30
Persecution and Peace	35
Constancy in Temptation	39
Unity through Humility	43
The Mind of Christ	46
The Spirit of Filial Obedience	50
The Call to Imitate Christ	54
The Presence of God	58
Sins of the Tongue	62
The Mystical Body in Action	65
The Chain of Tradition	70
How not to Imitate Christ	74
Imitating the Samaritan	79
Dying with Christ	86
Assimilation to Christ Crucified	90
Paul in Pursuit of Perfection	94
Citizens of a Better World	98
Jesus our Saviour	104
The Book of Life	107
Joy and Peace	110
Apostolic Poverty	114
Reunion of the Human Family	119

Appendices

1. The Place and Date of Composition of Philippians	122
2. The Text of the Epistle	124

Index

Gospel passages quoted	131

Foreword

This second book of Scripture for Meditation invites the reader to take St Paul's Epistle to the Philippians section by section and compare it with related passages from the gospels. Such comparisons have the incidental advantage of showing the continuity of St Paul's preaching with the preaching of Jesus, but the chief purpose here is to bring out more clearly the spiritual message of St Paul. The human mind reaches understanding in the process of comparison and contrast.

In the Reflections which follow the Scriptural texts I have tried to catch the inspiration of St Paul, in order to pass it on to others — rather as an ancient rhapsode would try to catch the spirit of a passage of Homer, to pass it on to his hearers. I have chosen the Epistle to the Philippians because it is an inspirational rather than a controversial writing, and because it reveals some of the gentler and more attractive traits in the Apostle's complex character.

John Bligh, S.J.

1
Readiness for Judgment

From Paul awaiting Judgment

Paul and Timothy, servants of Christ Jesus, to all who have been made holy in Christ Jesus at Philippi, and to your bishops and deacons: grace to you and peace from God our Father and from the Lord Jesus Christ.

I give thanks to my God for all your remembrance of me, always in all my prayers for you all, offering my prayer with joy over the share you have taken in spreading the gospel from the earliest days to the present time. I am confident that he who began this good work in you will continue to complete it until the Day of Christ Jesus. It is but right for me to think of you in this way, because you ever hold me in your hearts, when I am in prison, when I am on trial, when I am defending the gospel — you who are all sharers in the privilege granted to me. God is my witness, how I long for you all in the heart of Christ Jesus, and this is my prayer: that your love may abound more and more in all knowledge and discernment, so that you may always recognize what is better, and thus arrive faultless and blameless at the Lord's Assize, laden with the fruits of justice produced in you through Jesus Christ, for the glory and praise of God.

(Phil 1:1-11)

The Judgment awaiting All

When the Son of Man comes in his glory and all the angels with him, he will sit on his throne of glory and all the nations will be assembled before him. Then he will separate them out as a shepherd parts the sheep from the goats: he will make the sheep stand at his right and the goats at his left.

Then the King will say to those at his right: 'You whom my Father has blessed, come take possession of the kingdom that has been prepared for you from the foundation of the world. For I was hungry and you gave me food; I was thirsty and you gave me drink; I was a foreigner and you made me welcome; I was naked and you gave me clothes; I was ill and you looked after me; I was in prison and you visited me.' Then the just will reply: 'Lord, when did we see you hungry and give you food, or thirsty and give you drink? When did we see you a foreigner and make you welcome, or when did we see you naked and give you clothes? When did we see you ill or in prison and visit you?' Then the King will reply: 'I tell you truly, whatever you did for one of the lowliest of these my brothers, you did for me.'

Then he will speak to those on his left: 'You who are accursed: depart from me into the everlasting fire prepared for the devil and his angels. For I was hungry and you did not give me food; I was thirsty and you did not give me drink; I was a foreigner and you did not make me welcome; I was naked and you did not give me clothes; I was ill, and in prison, and you did not visit me.' Then they too will reply: 'Lord, when was it that we saw you hungry or thirsty or a foreigner or without clothing or ill or in prison, and did not help you?' And he will reply: 'I tell you truly, whatever you omitted to do for one of the lowliest of these, you omitted to do for me.' Then these will go away to everlasting punishment, but the just to everlasting life.

(*Mt 25:31-46*)

Reflection

St Paul is in prison, waiting to stand judgment before Caesar. In an ancient trial, the prosecution did not always confine itself to the one alleged crime; it often reviewed the whole of a man's life. St Paul is therefore expecting to have to render an account of his whole life before a human judge. If the case goes against him, he may soon afterwards have to stand before the tribunal of Christ. So his thought passes easily from the day of his trial to the Day of Christ. Both he and the Philippians will one day render their account to the Lord. The preaching of St Paul, like that of John the Baptist and of Christ himself, is dominated by the thought of Judgment, and of responsibility.

In the light of Judgment to come, St Paul looks back over the past. He says he is glad to see that the Philippians' fidelity has lasted out from the beginning to the present, and he prays that they will remain faithful from now until the end. He hopes that as they advance towards the Day of the Lord they will attain to an ever clearer understanding of God's will and to an ever greater perfection of charity, so that on the Day of the Lord they will be laden with the fruits of justice. He does not take the view that because they have been baptized and have received the Holy Spirit they are perfect already and their perseverance is assured. On the contrary, he knows their faults, as later sections of the Epistle will show, and he knows their need of encouragement. The Epistle was written partly for their instruction and exhortation. But it has another purpose too, as transpires at the very end: the Philippians have raised a sum of money and sent it to Paul by Epaphroditus, to alleviate the hardships of his imprisonment. Paul is sending Epaphroditus back, with a message of thanks (cf. 2:25). The gift of money is very welcome, yet causes Paul some embarrassment. However, he sees in it evidence of the Philippians' desire to share in his apostolic ministry and to produce the fruits of justice.

The passage from St Matthew gives us our Lord's own description of the Judgment, the Day of the Great Assize, which has also been called the Day of the Great Surprises. The Son of Man separates out the sheep from the goats; and the crucial question is not: 'Did you seek justification by faith alone?' but 'How did you treat the Son of Man in your neighbour? Did you care for the poor, the hungry, the foreigner, the prisoner?' Those who are condemned are condemned by the Son of Man, the new Adam, for their inhumanity to their fellow men. They lived selfishly, without caring for their neighbour. Some commentators have thought that the gospel scene refers especially to those who omitted to care for apostles and missionaries (like Paul) by contributing to their support and visiting them in prison.[1]

Here, then, is one important characteristic of a Christian community: we all believe in Judgment. When we look forward into the future, the perspective closes quite quickly, and at the point of junction is the seat of Judgment. This is the perspective of John the Baptist, of Christ our Lord, and of St Paul. Our time is short, it is not our own, we are responsible for how we use it.

---

[1] Cf. G.E. Ladd, *Jesus and the Kingdom,* London, 1965, p. 272.

This, however, is not a motive for anxiety — at least for men and women who are dedicated to corporal or spiritual works of mercy in the service of their fellow men. Christ our Lord and Saviour has begun a good work in us collectively and individually, and, as St Paul says, it is right for us to believe that God, who is faithful, will enable us to carry the work through to the end. In the first two chapters of the Epistle to the Romans, St Paul threatens the unbeliever with God's wrath on the Day of Judgment; but later in the same Epistle (8:28-34) he reassures the believer, saying in effect: 'God the Father took the first steps towards saving you before you were born, and he initiated the whole process with the serious intention of carrying it through: *he* predestined us, *he* called us, *he* justified us, and *he* will glorify us. At every stage the initiative rests with God rather than with man. When we appear before him for Judgment, we shall have nothing to fear. God the Father will be on our side, for, having given us his Son, what else will he not give and forgive? Christ our Lord will be on our side, for he died and rose to make intercession for us. And the Holy Spirit will be on our side, continuing his office of Advocate. But if God is for us, Father, Son and Holy Spirit, who will be against us?' All that we have to do is to show gratitude for God's goodness by prayers of thanksgiving and works of charity.

Prayer

O God our Father, who called us by your grace, we give thanks for your faithful love; and we pray that we may daily discern what is your will, and persevere in the service of our neighbour, until the Day when our lives will be judged by our Lord Jesus Christ, your Son, who lives and reigns with you in the unity of the Holy Spirit, and is God, for ever and ever.

2
Gratitude and Generosity

Grateful Giving

I give thanks to my God for all your remembrance of me, always in all my prayers for you all, offering my prayer with joy over the share you have taken in spreading the gospel from the earliest days to the present time. I am confident that he who began this good work in you will continue to complete it until the Day of Christ Jesus. It is but right for me to think of you in this way, because you ever hold me in your hearts, when I am in prison, when I am on trial, when I am defending the gospel — you who are all sharers in the privilege granted to me. *(Phil 1:3-7)*

Ungrateful Jealousy

A householder went out early in the morning to hire labourers for his vineyard. He made an agreement with the labourers that he would pay them a silver piece for the day's work, and sent them off into his vineyard. About nine o'clock, he went out again, and seeing some more men standing about idle in the market place, he said to them: 'You too, go into my vineyard, and I shall pay you a fair wage.' So off they went. Again about mid-day and at three in the afternoon, he went out and did the same. At last, about five o'clock, he went out and found still more men standing there; and he said to them: 'Why are you standing here idle all the day?' They replied: 'No one has hired us.' So he said to them: 'You too, go into the vineyard.'

When evening came, the owner of the vineyard said to his steward: 'Call the labourers and pay them their wages, beginning with the last and ending with the first.' Those hired at five o'clock came and received a silver piece. So when the first came, they expected to be paid more; but they too received the silver piece. At this they began to grumble against the owner: 'These last,' they said, 'have done only one hour's work, and you have treated them the same as us, who have been toiling all day in the heat.' In reply, the owner said to one of them: 'My friend, I do you no wrong. You settled with me for a silver piece, did you not? Then take your pay and be off. I mean to give the same to this last man as to you. Am I not allowed to do as I wish with what is my own? Or are you scowling because I am generous?'

(*Mt 20:1-15*)

Reflection

St Paul interprets the Philippians' gift not just as a mark of sympathy and compassion for himself personally, but as evidence that they wish to share in his God-given task of spreading the gospel. He calls it, not a 'task', but a 'grace' or 'privilege', and implies that they desire a share in this privilege. We do not know what motive was uppermost in the minds of the bishops and deacons who organized the collection, but we may suspect that St Paul is taking the opportunity to instruct them: a Christian ought to be keen and zealous to promote the further propagation of the gospel. If he is grateful for the gift of justification which faith has brought him, and if he appreciates God's grace at its true value, he will want others to share in so great a blessing.

However, people can be as jealous of their spiritual blessings and as unconcerned about their neighbour's spiritual good as they are jealous of their material prosperity and indifferent to his material poverty. In the parable of the Labourers in the Vineyard, Christ teaches a lesson which is applicable to both kinds of wealth. The owner of the vineyard is generous; and the workers, instead of being grateful, show themselves jealous.

The owner does not wish to send the late-comers home without a day's wage for the support of their families. Being a 'just' man, he pays them more than they have earned. (In the Bible, 'justice' normally implies compassion and mercy in addition to what we call 'justice'. Biblical justice is justice tempered with mercy and compassion.) But the workers hired in the early morning take a less liberal view. Instead of admiring the generosity of the owner, they murmur against him. They are more interested in preserving their 'differentials' than in seeing their neighbours treated as their brothers.

The owner rebukes them. Literally, his words are these: 'Is your eye evil because I am good?' — that is, 'Must you put on sour looks because I am generous?' However, the literal version has the advantage of echoing and recalling a passage on the same subject in the Sermon on the Mount, where Jesus says (Mt 6:22): 'If your eye is evil, your whole body will be in darkness.' A jealous, greedy person will live in gloom; the man whose eye shines with the light of generosity is the one who will live cheerfully and happily.

In the parable, the early workers are guilty of ordinary worldly jealousy over pay, but our Lord used the story as a warning to the scribes and Pharisees, who were guilty of spiritual jealousy. They were annoyed about the sinners whom Christ so easily forgave after they had spent half a lifetime in sin: were these people to be equal citizens in the kingdom with themselves who had struggled for years to keep the law of Moses?

The cure for both kinds of jealousy is gratitude — to count one's own blessings without comparing them with those given to others. Everyone has opportunities for jealousy, which are in fact temptations to sin. If we do not keep a watch over our thoughts, we can easily fall a prey to discontent: 'Why have I been passed over? Why was that job not given to me? Why do I have to work so hard for so little?' and so on. But this is folly. We should count the blessing which God has given us, beginning with our existence (it is said that a man's first heart attack reveals to him just how much he really loves his life), and then his redemption by Christ on the cross, his hopes of grace and glory... Gratitude is an essential part of our religious life.

But gratitude should express itself in generosity. It is not enough to admire the generosity of God. We should try to imitate it. That, says St Paul, is what the Philippians have done. They have received the blessings of the gospel. But they do not say: 'This is a good thing — let us keep it to ourselves; it gives us a superior wisdom.' (Some Christians at Corinth seem to have talked that way!) They recognized, at least implicitly: 'This is for everyone; let us help Paul to spread the gospel.' So they generously sent him money to provide for his needs.

Every Christian should share this generous impulse

to help the men through whom God sows the word of the gospel in fresh fields. Such generosity in turn strengthens the gratitude from which it springs.

Prayer

We give you thanks, O heavenly Father, for the gift of wisdom and of reconciliation which you have given us through Jesus Christ our Lord. Prosper the work of your missionaries in distant lands, and may they find encouragement in the assistance we send them.

3
Kinship in Christ

Heartfelt Love

I am confident that he who began this good work in you will continue to complete it until the Day of Christ Jesus. It is but right for me to think of you in this way, because *you ever hold me in your heart*, when I am in prison, when I am on trial, when I am defending the gospel — you who are all sharers in the privilege granted to me. God is my witness, how I long for you all in the heart of Christ Jesus. And this is my prayer: that your love may abound more and more in all knowledge and discernment. (*Phil 1:6-9*)

The phrase between asterisks is ambiguous in the Greek. It can mean 'You ever hold me in your heart' or 'I ever hold you in my heart.' St Paul delights in such ambiguities, and likes to profit by them.

The Heart of Christ

A large crowd was sitting round Jesus, and they said to him: "Look! Your mother and your brothers are outside, asking for you.' Jesus replied: 'Who is my mother? And who are my brothers?' Then he looked at the circle of those sitting round him and said: 'Here are my mother and my brothers! Whoever does the will of God is brother and sister and mother to me.'

(*Mk 3:32-35*)

Reflection

The Epistle to the Philippians has some of the characteristics of a love-letter. Its main purpose is not to communicate information or even instruction, but to give expression to Paul's gratitude and love for the Philippians, and to foster their love for one another and for him.

In the opening passage, he uses some very affectionate words. He and they share in one grace and are united by such a strong bond of love that he can say to them: 'I long for you all', or, as we should say: 'I miss you terribly.' In the continuation of this phrase there may be an allusion to a great mystery: 'I long for you all in the entrails of Christ Jesus', or, as we would say nowadays, 'in the heart of Christ Jesus.' Already St Paul may be thinking of Christ as the Second Adam (he certainly does so later, in chapter 2): Christ is in Paul and Christ is in the Philippians, as Adam was in himself and in Eve who was taken from his side. As Adam yearned for the flesh of his flesh and she for him, so the members of Christ yearn for one another. The word which St Paul uses of his 'longing' is one which can be used of the attraction of the sexes. He takes it up and transfers it to a higher plane: 'I long for you in the heart of Jesus.'

The passage from St Mark shows that it was Christ's intention to unite his disciples into a family of brothers and sisters — a family resting not on blood, nor on the will of man, but on the word of God accepted with faith and obedience. The early Christians called one another 'brother' and 'sister' to express the love which God put into their hearts for one another.

St Paul's words also tell us something important about his prayer: the thought of his friends and his strong affection for them were not excluded from his mind when he turned to God. On the contrary, the warm affection which he felt when he remembered them in prayer helped to kindle his love for Christ and for God the Father. Love of God and love of man cannot be dissociated from each other, even in prayer. 'He who does not love his brother whom he has seen cannot love God whom he has not seen' (1 Jn 4:20). Prayer is not likely to be an exercise of heartfelt love for God, if human persons are shut out of mind. Our friends have a necessary place in our prayer.

Prayer

Heavenly Father, you have access into the inmost heart of . . . and . . . and . . . whom I dearly love. Fill them with light and love, so that they may find consolation in your presence and serve you with joy. Teach them and me to recognize at every turning-point what is the better thing — what is true, venerable, just and holy.

4

The Suffering Servant

All is for the Best

I want you to know, brethren, that my situation here has turned out to be more of a help than a hindrance to the progress of the gospel. Everyone in the fortress, and outside as well, has come to know that I am imprisoned for Christ's sake. And most of our brethren in the Lord have been encouraged by my imprisonment to show even greater boldness in preaching the word of God — some through envy and ambition, others with a good will. Those who proclaim Christ out of love, do so because they know that I am confined here for the defence of the gospel; the others, not for any holy motive, but out of rivalry — they think to cause me further affliction in my imprisonment. But why should I mind, so long as one way or another, whether sincerely or for less worthy motives, Christ is being preached. Meanwhile, I am in good spirits and shall continue to be so, because I am convinced that this whole affair will end with my liberation, through your prayers. *(Phil 1:12-19)*

Justice will Triumph

Jesus entered a synagogue, and among those present was a man with a withered hand. They put to Jesus the question: 'Does the law allow curing on the sabbath?' For they wanted a charge to bring against him. He replied: 'Which of you, if he has a sheep that falls into a pit on the sabbath, will not take hold of it and pull it out? Yet surely a man is much more valuable than a sheep! The law does allow one to do good on the sabbath.' Then he said to the man: 'Stretch out your hand.' He did so, and the hand was restored and made as sound as the other. Then the Pharisees went out and plotted against him, to make an end of him.

Jesus knew of this and left the place. Large numbers followed him, and he cured all their sick; but he charged them not to make him known, in order that the word might be fulfilled which was spoken by the prophet Isaiah when he said: 'Behold my Servant whom I have chosen, my beloved, in whom my soul is well pleased; I shall put my Spirit upon him, and he will proclaim Judgment to the Gentiles. He will not wrangle nor cry out, and no one will hear his voice in the streets. He will not break the crushed reed; he will not snuff the smoking wick. At length he will bring justice to victory; and the Gentiles will place their hope in his name.'

(Mt 12:9-21)

Reflection

In this section of the Epistle, St Paul is consoling the Philippians, and reassuring them. They must not be distressed about his imprisonment, or let it give rise to any doubts about his vocation as an apostle or about God's providence. They must not, for example, say to themselves: 'How can God allow his apostle to be cooped up in prison, instead of going about preaching the gospel? Can it be that Paul is mistaken in thinking he is an apostle? Could God allow a true apostle to be cooped up like that?' To all such doubts and questionings St Paul replies: 'Unexpectedly, my imprisonment has turned out for the better: all the soldiers in the garrison — men whom otherwise the gospel could not have reached — all have heard about the gospel; and outside the prison the other Christians are preaching more boldly.'

Apparently some of them, animated by Paul's courage, were trying to carry on from where he had been compelled to leave off; but others, he says, were moved by jealousy — which is puzzling. Presumably some preachers were saying: 'Now that Paul is out of the way, we can take the lead in this new movement. He imagines that he is indispensable for the preaching of the gospel; let us show him that he is not — by winning more converts than he ever won. God is teaching him how unnecessary he is by shutting him up in prison. He is getting what he deserves for his boasting.' St Paul has heard of these jealousies, but he refuses to be upset. What does it matter, he says, so long as the gospel is preached? Even when it is preached from unworthy motives of self-advertisement or ambition, the gospel still contains the power of God unto salvation: God is able to make not only the hostility of our enemies but even the failings of our friends work together for his purpose.

There is no exact parallel in the life of Christ himself. We have no reason to think that he was ever imprisoned during the public ministry. Indeed when threatened by danger, he was sometimes miraculously preserved (cf. Lk 4:30; Jn 8:20). But the passage from Matthew 12 shows that Jesus too became the object of intense jealousy and unreasoning enmity, and was prevented by his enemies from preaching freely. St Matthew points out that he took it in the spirit of the Suffering Servant described by Isaiah, and just went along, unobtrusively, curing the sick, waiting for the time when his Father would bring justice to victory. Another story which would illustrate this well is the Rejection in Samaria described at the end of Luke 9 — when the Samaritans refused to give Jesus lodging because his face was set towards Jerusalem. James and John, the sons of thunder, said: 'Do you want us to call down fire from heaven and destroy them?' But Jesus replied: 'You do not know of what spirit you are!' And the text concludes, very quietly, 'he left the place and went to another village.'

Christ our Lord recognised that he must fulfil the part of the Suffering Servant — a role of patience. So too did St Paul. He several times speaks of his own vocation in phrases borrowed from the Servant Songs. He never says very clearly that *all* Christians are called to share the fate of the Servant; and yet presumably it must be so, because Christ called upon all his followers to take up their cross and follow him.

Therefore every Christian should *expect* to meet with a certain amount of hostility and jealousy and disappointment — and of opposition even from his brothers within the Church. When this occurs, the natural reaction is to become angry, to rebel, and to call down fire from heaven. (That can be done in a number of ways which need not be specified here!) But the true Christian will show the same quiet strength and cheerful acceptance as St Paul, trying to see the hand of God in all things; and he will go along unobtrusively doing good, as Christ did, while the trouble blows over. In the nature of things, virtue cannot grow strong without being put to the test. One cannot become like St Paul, or like Christ, without experiencing some taste of opposition, jealousy and misunderstanding, and accepting these things with courage and cheerfulness, composure and self-control. That too is a part of the Christian spirit, and not the easiest part to make one's own.

Prayer

O God our Father, whose providence never fails, lead us not into temptation; but when trials and temptations come, grant that we may discern your will in them, and welcome them with patience and cheerfulness. Through our Lord Jesus Christ, your Son, who lives and reigns with you in the unity of the Holy Spirit, and is God, for ever and ever.

5
Pain and Joy

The Privilege of Suffering

I give thanks to my God for all your remembrance of me, always in all my prayers for you all, offering my prayer with joy over the share you have taken in spreading the gospel from the earliest days to the present time....It is but right for me to think of you in this way, because you ever hold me in your hearts, when I am in prison, when I am on trial, when I am defending the gospel — you who are sharers in the *privilege* granted to me. God is my witness, how I long for you all in the heart of Jesus Christ — and this is my prayer: that your love may abound more and more in all knowledge and discernment. *(Phil 1:3-9)*

The Way to Glory

Judas took the piece of bread and at once went out; and it was night. When he had gone out, Jesus said: 'Now is the Son of Man glorified, and God is glorified in him! If God is glorified in him, God will also glorify him in himself; and he will do so without delay.'

(Jn 13:30-32)

Reflection

Before passing on from the subject of suffering, it will be profitable to go back to a sentence in the opening section of the Epistle, where there is a significant divergence between the Latin Vulgate and the original Greek. In the Greek text, St Paul describes the Philippians as sharers in the 'grace' or 'privilege' (*charitos*) that is given him. But in the Latin version they are described as sharers in the 'joy' that is his. No doubt the Latin version was made from a defective Greek manuscript which read *charas* ('joy') in place of *charitos;* but the Latin makes very good sense, for St Paul goes on to say that, as things are turning out, he is *glad* to be suffering in prison. If the Philippians have attained to full knowledge and understanding, they will share in his spiritual joy.

St Paul is speaking of a joy which does not banish pain but transforms it. Just as the prophet Isaiah during the Exile felt the pain, the privations and the humiliation of being uprooted from his home and country, yet was able to accept these things as God's will and as serving a good purpose, so too with Paul: he finds it possible to rejoice over his imprisonment.

We do not need much imagination, or much experience of suffering, to enable us to recognize that for one who is able to accept willingly and even joyfully the privations and hardships of prison or exile, suffering can be a wonderful means of purification. Such a sufferer still feels anguish in his heart, and still longs for his friends and home, but instead of becoming rebellious or bitter, he accepts his lot, and even rejoices over it, because once accepted, it is an aid to justice and holiness for himself and for others. He can rejoice over the opportunity granted him to make amends for past waywardness (cf. Jn 21:18).

In the life of Jesus, the homelessness, incomprehension, hostility and failure which he suffered were not a means of purification, since there was no evil in him to be cleansed away. Yet even for him suffering was a means of refinement or perfection, as the Epistle to the Hebrews teaches us (cf. Heb 2:10). He too rejoiced over the sufferings which his Father's will assigned to him. On the night before his trial, when Judas went out into the night to betray him, he uttered a cry of exultation: 'Now is the Son of Man glorified, and God is glorified in him!'

In every man's life there is a measure of suffering. Disappointment and privations are the lot of every son of man. If these things are neither understood nor accepted, they produce bitterness; but if understood and even welcomed, they foster a degree of holiness which cannot be reached by any other way. St Paul prays that the Philippians may abound in all knowledge. One of the most important things which a Christian has to learn is the value of suffering and the wisdom of accepting the cross. If he has this knowledge, sufferings and privations will supply fuel for spiritual joy. The bitter-sweetness of suffering accepted with patience as a gift from the hands of God will help him to arrive purified and faultless at the judgment seat of Christ, for the glory and praise of God.

Prayer

Grant us the wisdom, O heavenly Father, to accept gladly what we cannot change, and to welcome the sufferings of our lives for the purification of our souls, in union with the passion of our Lord Jesus Christ your Son, who lives and reigns with you in the unity of the Holy Spirit, and is God, for ever and ever.

6

Detachment

Stingless Death

I am confident that this whole affair will end with my liberation, through your prayers and through an abundant outpouring of the Spirit of Jesus Christ. For it is my hope and expectation that far from being put to shame, I shall speak out confidently, so that Christ will be glorified, now as always, in my person — whether I am to live, or whether I am to die. For, so far as I am concerned, to live is Christ, and to die will be a gain. But if to live on in the flesh means that I shall do fruitful work, then I do not know what to choose. I am pulled in two directions, longing to depart this life and be with Christ (which is far the better thing); and yet, for your sake, it is more expedient that I should remain in the flesh. Therefore I am confident that I shall stay and stand by you all, to sustain your progress and your joy in the faith. Then you will have even greater confidence in Christ Jesus on my account, at my return (*parousia*) to be with you. (*Phil 1:19-26*)

Unwelcome Death

There was a rich man whose farm produced large crops. He thought to himself: 'What am I to do? I have no room to store my crops.' Then he said: 'I know: I will pull down my barns and build larger ones and store all my grain and goods in them. Then I shall say to myself: "Now you have plenty of good things stored up for many a year; take your ease, eat, drink and enjoy yourself." ' But God said to him: 'Foolish man! This very night your life is forfeit; and the goods you have amassed, whose will they be?' (*Lk 12:16-20*)

Reflection

This passage of the Epistle contains a fine expression of Christian detachment. Although St Paul is facing trial and may be sentenced to death, he is not anxious. He has faced death in his mind, and has accepted it. From his own personal point of view, he would even prefer to die, in order to be with Christ. For him, to die would mean a gain of life, not a loss. Just as Christ at the Last Supper looked forward to being with the Father, and prayed for his disciples 'that where I am they also may be, that they may see my glory,' so Paul is capable of looking beyond death and desiring to be with Christ and see his glory — again, as on the road to Damascus. However, he says, if there is still a task to be done on this earth, for the good of the Philippians, to strengthen their faith, and to help them find joy in their faith, then he is willing to stay on this earth for a while. On balance, he thinks it likely that he will return to Philippi.

In the Greek, he playfully describes his eventual return as a *parousia*. He looks forward to this joyful encounter with his friends as a visible image of his heavenly hope. But he no longer expects to see the visible return of Christ in his own lifetime; he will depart this life and go to be with Christ (cf. 3:20).

How different is the Apostle's view of death from the death of the Rich Fool who lives for this world alone! For the Fool, death is the ruin of all his hopes and ambitions; for Paul it is the gateway to fulfilment. We can see in this contrast something of what he meant when he said that death has lost its sting: 'To die will be a gain.'

Two further contrasts may be helpful here. To the psalmist death caused horror because it meant being cut off from God: in Sheol the dead no longer praise him (cf. Ps 30:9); death meant reduction to a shadowy existence which could not be called life. For the Christian, St Paul says, the contrary is true: death will mean a 'gain' of life and closer union with God in the presence of Christ.

Secondly, to the modern unbeliever death means extinction; it is often compared to being snuffed out like a candle — something neither particularly terrible, nor on the other hand attractive, just a brute fact, best not thought about. There is a whimsical saying of Maurice Chevalier that 'old age is not so bad when you consider the alternative.' For the Christian there are two alternatives, and extinction is not one of them. The one he should hope for is to be with Christ — a condition much more desirable than unserviceable old age. For St Paul, as he grows older, departure from this world has become positively desirable.

And meanwhile, he says, 'for me, to live is Christ!' If the Epistle was written during the Roman captivity, towards the close of St Paul's life, or even if it was written a few years earlier during an Ephesian imprisonment,[1] it is a remarkable exclamation, because St Paul

---
[1] See the Appendix below, pp. 122-123.

is not a young man, and yet it is a cry of youthful enthusiasm. Paul still finds joy and excitement in being a Christian. 'To live is Christ!' — he means: 'Life would be dull, flat, boring, if we had not Christ to live for, Christ to imitate, to talk about, to feel like an atmosphere in which we live and move and have our being. Without him we should be reduced to trivialities, to the vain repetitions and empty wisdom of the Gentiles, and in that case life would be a tiresome burden.'

To many quite good Christians, St Paul's words sound a trifle extravagant. 'To live is Christ!' — why, it is not even good grammar! But it was certainly true. If St Paul had not been an apostle of Christ, what would he have had to say to the Philippians? He would have been just a Jewish tourist, or an immigrant tradesman. But Christ brought him into a new, joyful, personal union with these people, which gave meaning and warmth to their lives and his, and created a strong bond of affection. Take away Christ, and Paul's world would have been cold and empty.

People who are dedicated to any form of apostolic endeavour should not find St Paul's words too extravagant. And yet (I think) we often do — which is a sign that we have surrendered our detachment. But we can always regain it through the exercise of prayer. Today let us hear the Lord's voice in these words of Scripture and try again to detach our hearts from this world as completely as ever in the past. Let us be bold enough to pray as follows.

Prayer

Lord, if it is your will, I am ready to die today; or if not, if there is still some task for me to do here, well and good. But thy kingdom come on earth! Fill me with the Holy Spirit, and fill all my friends with the Holy Spirit, so that we may recapture the joy which those early Christians found in their faith. Come, Lord Jesus, and fill the vacant spaces in our hearts. Marana tha! Come, Lord, and lodge in our hearts, or, the other way around, let us lodge in yours.

7
Persecution and Peace

The Promised Advocate

I am confident that this whole affair will end with my liberation, through your prayers and through an abundant outpouring of the Spirit of Jesus Christ. For it is my hope that far from being put to shame, I shall speak out confidently, so that Christ will be glorified, now as always, in my person, whether I am to live, or whether I am to die. *(Phil 1:19-20)*

A Blessing in Disguise

I am the true Vine, and my Father is the Vine-dresser. Those of my branches that do not bear fruit, he cuts off; and those which do bear fruit, he prunes, so that they will yield still more. You are clean already, by reason of the word that I have spoken to you. Remain in me, and I shall remain in you. A branch cannot yield its fruit unless it remains on the vine, and no more can you, unless you remain attached to me. I am the Vine, you are the branches. The man who remains attached to me, and I to him, he it is who yields fruit in plenty; for apart from me you can do nothing. He who does not remain attached to me is thrown out like a broken branch and withers; and withered branches are gathered up, thrown on the fire and burned. If you remain attached to me, and my words remain in you, ask whatever you wish, and it will be done for you. (*Jn 15:1-7*)

Reflection

St George was chosen patron of England in an age when warfare was much more glamorous than it is now. We are no longer a nation of warriors. St Thomas More is better suited to be our patron now. It is sometimes said, however, that the whole idea of patron saints is out of date — that it is a relic of a period of history, the decadence of the Roman Empire, when it was impossible to get anything done in the world unless you had a friend at court who would put in a good word for you with the Emperor. Certainly we must not suppose that the government of the universe is run on those lines; and it is noticeable that St Paul does not say: 'If I die, it will be a gain to you, because I shall intercede for you in the Lord's presence.' The gain he mentions is for himself. However, he clearly values the intercession of the Philippian 'saints' while they live. If death will mean a gain of life to them, there seems no reason why their intercession should not have enhanced value when they are with the Lord. We should not, therefore, abandon the practice of invoking the intercession of the saints — especially as all that we say to them, God overhears.

What warfare is to the secular world, persecution is to the Church. Warfare brings out the best in men as well as the worst; and persecution too, though it has always caused a shocking number of apostasies, can be a source of blessings, as Christ says in the passage about the Vine. When Christians are persecuted, they must say to themselves: 'God the Father is pruning his vine, to make it bear more fruit.'

Just as many a man in the secular world has longed for the opportunity to distinguish himself or make a clean exit from the world on the battlefield, so many Christians in the early centuries wanted to undergo persecution and martyrdom. St Paul in prison tells the Philippians that he is looking forward to his trial, because he is sure that when brought before his judge, thanks to their intercession, he will have the special aid of the Holy Spirit, as Jesus promised. St Ignatius of Antioch went further: he wrote to his friends in Rome and asked them not to intervene at court on his behalf, because he wanted to be ground to pieces by the jaws of lions for the sake of Christ. Some early Christians went even further and provoked pagan judges by insulting their false gods.

Nowadays, we are ashamed of warfare as a subhuman way of settling disputes, and we are still more ashamed of religious persecution. We must learn to live without both. But that means we must live without the gifts of the Spirit that belong to times of trial and crisis. We must learn to endure the test of prolonged peace. When the state and the Church are threated by an external enemy, unity, charity and heroism come much more easily. Ours is the difficult task of finding these things in the midst of peace. How can it be done? It is hard to say, but here is one suggestion: that our biggest battles are to be fought in prayer. In times of prayer, we must foresee the occasions when we shall be tempted, and overcome them beforehand, in prayer.

One of the most revealing incidents in the life of St Thomas More occurred on the morning when he was going by the river from Chelsea to Westminster, with his son-in-law Roper, to face the King's commissioners. For a long time he sat silent. Then he broke the silence by saying: 'Thank God, son Roper, the field is won.' He conquered his fear and his enemies beforehand, in prayer and meditation.

Prayer

Grant, O heavenly Father, that we who live in a time of peace and toleration, may not lack the aid of your Holy Spirit. Inspire us to serve you loyally in peace as your saints and martyrs did in times of persecution. May we be helped by their example and intercession.

8
Constancy in Temptation

A Warning to Unbelievers

Be sure that the life of your community is worthy of the gospel, so that whether I come and see you or receive news of you at a distance, I may know that you are standing firm, united in spirit, battling with one soul through faith in the gospel, and refusing to be in any way put out by your enemies. To them your constancy is a warning of their doom, granted by God; to you it is a pledge of your salvation — that you have been granted the privilege of taking Christ's side, not only by believing in him, but also by suffering for him, sharing the same trials which you once saw me undergo and now hear that I am undergoing again. *(Phil 1:27-30)*

A Warning to Paul

Stephen said: 'You, my hearers, are the same as your fathers. Stiff-necked and uncircumcised in heart and ears, you have always resisted the Holy Spirit. Was there one of the prophets whom your fathers did not persecute? They put to death those who foretold the coming of the Just One, whom you have now betrayed and murdered — you who received the law at the angels' bidding, but have not kept it.'

When they heard this, they were stung to fury and ground their teeth at him. But Stephen, filled with the Holy Spirit, gazed up into heaven and saw the glory of God and Jesus standing at God's right hand. He cried out: 'Look! I see heaven opened and the Son of Man standing at God's right hand!' But they raised loud shouts and stopped their ears and all rushed at him together. Then they threw him out of the city and stoned him. The witnesses placed their cloaks at the feet of a young man named Saul. While Stephen was being stoned, he cried out in prayer: 'Lord Jesus, receive my spirit!' Then he fell to his knees and cried in a loud voice: 'Lord, do not reckon this sin against them!' And so saying, he fell asleep in death. Saul had been one of those who approved of the killing of Stephen.

(Acts 7:51—8:1) [1]

Reflection

The most striking thought in this passage of the Epistle is in the sentence, 'You have been granted the privilege of suffering for Christ.' It is a privilege to share the fate of our Lord himself and to have an opportunity to become like him through suffering. The perfection which he attained through suffering cannot be attained by his followers without suffering. Further, to share Christ's sufferings is a pledge of salvation, for he will never prove

---

[1] Those who use these selections for the liturgy can substitute Mk 8:34-38 for this second reading.

less faithful than those who have proved themselves faithful to him. One who has preached may still become a castaway, but one who has suffered for him has stronger grounds of hope (cf. Rom 5:3-5).

The sufferings which give to the faithful a pledge of salvation are at the same time a warning to their persecutors that if they persist in their hostility, they will perish. St Paul is drawing on his own experience here. In the days when he persecuted Christians, his conscience began to trouble him. When he saw the spirit of forgiveness in which Stephen died,[1] he must have felt misgivings. Not long afterwards, the Lord told him not to kick against the goad (Acts 26:14). Now in his prison, he finds that his own patience in the midst of suffering is commending the gospel to everyone in the garrison (cf. 1:13). He therefore urges the Philippians to stand firm in their faith, so that they too will shine out as a beacon in the world, and offer to unbelievers the word of life (cf. 2:15-16).

In a time like the present, when most Christians are not undergoing persecution, we must still endure the silent opposition and disapproval of the world. If our life is worthy of the gospel, the world will hate or at least dislike us because we are not of the world, and will constantly tempt us to adopt its own permissive ways and lax standards. Even in times of peace, Christians live in the midst of temptations. Therefore St Paul's exhortation is always relevant: if we wish to fulfil the destiny to which God is calling us, we must recognize temptation and stand firm. When the patriarch Joseph was tempted by Potiphar's wife, if he had succumbed, he would not have become the ruler of Egypt. When Moses was sent to speak to Pharoah, if he had flinched

---

[1] He was consciously imitating the Lord — cf. Lk 23:34. Contrast the dying words of Zacharias in 2 Chron 24:22: 'The Lord look upon it and require it.'

before his anger, he would not have become the leader of the Israelites. Both these men feared the divine King whom they could not see more than the human king whom they could see (cf. Heb 11:27). The Philippians are told not to fear their earthly enemies (1:28), but to fear God who is invisibly at work amongst them (2:12). Such is the faith which is required of all Christians in temptations of whatever kind. If we fail in the few great temptations which dot our lives, God in his goodness may allow us to repent, but we have no right to expect that he will still give us the graces and privileges which he would have given, had we overcome.

Prayer

O God, our Saviour and Protector, give us strength in adversity and constancy in temptation, so that our fidelity may be a warning to others and a petition for further opportunities to serve you. Lead us not into temptation, but deliver us from evil.

9
Unity through Humility

Paul the Peacemaker

If a word of encouragement in Christ, if an appeal made in love, if fellowship in the Spirit, if tenderness and compassion have any power with you, bring my joy to completion by being all of one mind, united in one love, living by one soul, sharing one mind. Do nothing from jealousy or empty ambition; be humble; believe, each of you, that the others are better than you are; look to your neighbour's interest rather than to your own. Let there be one mind in you, the mind of Christ.

(Phil 2:1-5)

Jesus the Peacemaker

The mother of the sons of Zebedee came to Jesus with her sons, and fell on her knees and begged a favour of him. He replied: 'What is your wish?' She said: 'Promise that in your kingdom these two sons of mine may sit one on your right and one on your left.' Jesus answered: 'You do not know what you are asking. Can you drink the chalice that I am to drink?' They answered: 'We can.' He said to them: 'You will indeed drink of my chalice; but to sit on my right or left is not mine to give; it belongs to those for whom my Father has reserved it.'

When the other ten heard about this, they were indignant with the two brothers. But Jesus called them all to him and said: 'You know how the rulers of the Gentiles lord it over their subjects, and their great men reign like tyrants. It shall not be so among you. Whoever wants to be first among you must be the slave of all — like the Son of Man, who has not come to be served, but to serve, and to offer his life as a ransom for many.'
(*Mt 20:20-28*)

Reflection

Earlier in the Epistle (1:17), St Paul mentioned certain deplorable jealousies, rivalries and divisions within the church of Rome — or of Ephesus, if the Epistle was written from there.[1] These troubles make him think: 'How unworthy of the gospel! May the church of Philippi never fall into this wretched condition!' But alas! he *has* heard of some tension or misunderstanding between two women of Philippi, Evodia and Syntyche (cf. 4:2). So he appeals to the whole church of Philippi, warmly and affectionately, to preserve the unity which should be the mark of a Christian congregation: there should be no rivalries, jealousies or divisions, but one soul, one love, one spirit, uniting all. A united church, in which there is no grumbling against authority and no disputing about doctrine will shine out as a beacon in

---

[1] See the Appendix below, pp. 122-123.

the world (cf. 2:14-15), and will be a portent of the consummation to which the whole universe is moving, when every being in heaven, on earth and under the earth will unite in acclaiming the Lordship of Christ.

When St Paul expressed the hope that the Philippians would learn to discern and recognize what is better (1:10), he did not at once explain what he had in mind. Now it appears that he wants them to recognize among other things that humility is better than rivalry, and unselfish concern for others is better than personal ambition. These are the Christlike virtues which preserve and foster unity. If the Philippians have within them a perceptive, sensitive heart, a heart inhabited by the Spirit of Christ, they will heed Paul's exhortation and bring his joy to completion by being all of one mind.

The secret of unity is simple, yet Christians have rarely succeeded in mastering it: unity is preserved by humility, which consists, not in self-contempt, but in deference to others and willingness to serve them. Nothing is so destructive of love, affection, unity and peace as pride and the jealousies, rivalries and ambitions that are born of pride. That is also the lesson of the gospel passage: the ambition of the sons of Zebedee provokes a quarrel among the apostles, and Christ heals the situation by a lesson in humility. There is no incident in the gospel which better illustrates the beatitude, 'Blessed are the peacemakers.' The peacemakers are those who, like Christ himself, appreciate the value of humility, and prefer to serve, because they know it is better.

Prayer

Give us the wisdom, O heavenly Father, to set aside ambition and devote ourselves to the service of our neighbour, in imitation of Jesus Christ your Son our Lord, who offered his life as a ransom for us.

10

The Mind of Christ

The Great Reversal

Be of one mind. Do nothing from jealousy or empty ambition; but in all humility believe, each of you, that the others are better than you are; look to your neighbour's interest, not to your own. Let there be one mind in you, the mind of Christ, who, being in the form of God, did not make it his ambition to be treated as God, but emptied himself, and took the form of a servant. He was born in the manner of men, and wearing the appearance of man, he humbled himself, and was obedient unto death, even to death on a cross. Therefore God exalted him greatly, and bestowed on him the name that is above all names, so that in the name of Jesus every knee shall bend, in heaven, on earth, and under the earth, and every tongue shall acclaim Jesus Christ as Lord, to the glory of God his Father. (*Phil 2:3-11*)

Silent Night

While they were there, Mary's time was fulfilled, and she

brought forth a son, her firstborn, and wrapped him in swaddling clothes, and laid him in a manger, as there was no room for them at the inn.

There were shepherds in that country, out in the open, keeping the night-watches over their flocks. And behold, an angel of the Lord appeared above them, and the glory of the Lord shone about them, and they were greatly afraid. But the angel said to them: 'Have no fear. For behold, I bring you a gospel of great joy for all the people: a Saviour has been born for you this night, in the city of David. He is the Lord Messiah. This will be the sign: you will find a child wrapped in swaddling clothes and laid in a manger.' Then suddenly there appeared with the angel a great throng of the heavenly army praising God and singing: 'Glory to God on high, and on earth peace to men of his good pleasure.'
(*Lk 2:6-14*)

Reflection

Both St Paul and St Luke are moved to write poetry, when they contemplate the wonderful mystery of the Incarnation of God's Son. He was born in the manner of men, the firstborn of his mother, and wrapped in swaddling clothes, and the little bundle was laid in a manger — an unusual cradle for a new born babe, and an easy sign for the shepherds to recognize. But that is not the only point of the swaddling clothes and the manger. The ass has its stable and the ox its manger, but the Son of Man has nowhere of his own to lay his head. He is born in another man's stable, and buried in another man's tomb.[1] The beginning of his earthly life is like the end — and like the middle too, when he said to the prospective disciple that foxes have their holes

---

[1] For further resemblances, see *Scripture for Meditation, 1: The Infancy Narratives,* pp. 41-42.

and the birds of the air their nests (Mt 8:20). He is a visitor from another world, destined one day to be the Lord of all, but content for the time being to be more homeless than Abraham, a sojourner in the promised land, a pilgrim on the way to the heavenly Jerusalem.

This is how God chose to come into the world. Still today, though we have read the story so often, who does not wince with amazement to think that this child is the Lord Messiah, the fulfilment of the hope of Israel! And this is how he comes!

He comes in complete poverty — not in a house, nor even in an inn, but outside in a stable. Yet poverty does not make the scene sad or squalid. On the contrary, there is an unearthly beauty and joy and serenity in its atmosphere, which we must first inhale, and then learn a lesson. We are called upon to imitate Christ in his humility, poverty, emptiness; and if we will only try to do it, this unearthly peace and joy can be renewed in us. Even small self-sacrifices, inspired by the memory of his big one, are often rewarded with unaccountably generous consolations of the spirit.

This is really the lesson which St Paul is drawing. He is saying: Imitate Christ our Lord in emptying yourself, taking the form of a servant, and serving one another in charity, because this is the bond of peace. True, we were not in the form of God to start with; but we can put aside the halo of pride and self-admiration, and accept the status of a servant, of a satellite, of a poor man who regards others as more important than himself. If this is the mind of each member, how firmly a community will be knit together in bonds of peace and serenity!

Those who share with the sons of Zebedee the desire to distinguish themselves in Christ's service are promised in both these texts that if they will empty out their pride completely, and renounce the worldly goods which bolster it, the Holy Spirit will come upon them, and God will begin to use them in a new way, to praise him, to adore him, to serve him. If we had practical knowledge of humility and knew the taste of real poverty, we might be able to relax and let the Holy Spirit pray within us, so that, for example the actual words we use when reciting the *Gloria* would be something like the doodling a man does while he is thinking. May God instruct us!

Blessed are the poor in spirit. But spiritual poverty can hardly be achieved without some experience of real poverty.

Prayer

Almighty God, Father of our Lord Jesus Christ, who sent forth your firstborn Son to take the form of a servant, grant that we too, his brethren, may find joy in a life of humility, poverty and service. Pour out upon us a spirit of prayer, so that our minds may rest effortlessly in adoration of your beloved Son, our Lord, who lives and reigns with you in the unity of the Holy Spirit, God, for ever and ever.

11
The Spirit of Filial Obedience

Jesus the Second Adam

Let there be one mind in you, the mind of Christ, who, being in the form of God, did not make it his ambition to be treated as God, but emptied himself, and took the form of a servant. He was born in the manner of men, and wearing the appearance of man, he humbled himself, and was obedient unto death, even to death on a cross. Therefore God exalted him greatly, and bestowed on him the name that is above all names, so that in the name of Jesus every knee shall bend, in heaven, on earth, and under the earth, and every tongue shall acclaim Jesus Christ as Lord, to the glory of God his Father.
(Phil 2:5-11)

Jesus the Son of God

From mid-day darkness covered the whole land until three; and at three Jesus cried out in a loud voice: 'Eli,

Eli, lama sabachthani?' (that is, 'My God, my God, why hast thou forsaken me?') Some of the bystanders heard this and said: 'Do you hear? He is calling Elijah!' But one of them quickly soaked a sponge in sharp wine, fixed it on a cane, and held it up for Jesus to drink. 'Wait!' he cried, 'Let us see if Elijah comes to take him down.' Then Jesus gave a loud cry and died. When the centurion, who was standing facing him, saw that he had died in this way, he said: 'This was indeed God's Son.'

(*Mk 15:33-39*)

Reflection

At the time of writing this Epistle, St Paul was facing trial and perhaps death. It was inevitable that in these circumstances he should meditate on the passion and death of Christ. Inevitable too that he should compare his own life with the life of Christ, to see how far his own conformed to the pattern set before him.

He saw the life of Christ as a progressive self-emptying, and he noted the contrast between the first Adam and the second. The first Adam, and Eve, desired to be as God, knowing good and evil, that is, they desired to be autonomous, deciding for themselves what is good and bad, right and wrong.[1] But the second Adam did not make it his ambition to be treated as God, or honoured as God, though he was God. Instead, he became obedient and emptied himself. The Incarnation was a Transfiguration in reverse. Our Lord put aside his glory and took the form of a slave; and that was not enough — he became obedient unto death, and to one of the most frightful forms of death which men in their cruelty have devised. He was rejected by his own people,

---

[1] See the note (by R. de Vaux) on Genesis 2:17 in *The Jerusalem Bible*.

handed over to the hated Romans, led out of the city, stripped of his garments, raised up off the earth, spread-eagled; and when he died, a spear was thrust through his side to complete his self-emptying.

The same pattern had been repeated, to some extent, in the life of Paul. All that had been his pride in his youth and early manhood — his pure Jewish blood, his observance of the law, his standing as a rabbi — all these things he had emptied out as so much rubbish at a sign of God's will. He too suffered rejection by his own people, imprisonments, accusations before the Roman governor; and here he was in prison awaiting trial. The emptying-out was almost complete; and he finds the courage to say, a little later in the Epistle, that if the last drops of his life must be poured out in sacrifice, he is glad.

He has learned, and tries to pass on to the Philippians, the lesson of Christ's passion, which is the lesson of obedience, of accepting God's will mediated by human authorities both good and bad. Our Lord during his lifetime submitted to human authority at its most gentle (when he was a child in the care of his mother) and at its most brutal (when Pilate gave him up to appease the angry crowd). He submitted because it was his Father's will. He said so obscurely to his mother at the age of twelve, and less obscurely to Pilate during his trial: 'You would not have any power over me, if it had not been given you from above.' But because Pilate was invested with power from above, he submitted and obeyed, like a servant. 'Not my will, but thine be done,' he said during the struggle in Gethsemane; then, all through his passion, in spite of intense provocations, he retained his calm.

Job's wife said to her husband in his misery: 'Curse God and die!' If the devil had been able to draw Jesus into bitter and resentful thoughts or words against the

Jews, or his executioners, or against God who had willed all this, the devil would have won the contest. But the heart of Jesus went through this fiery trial without any trace of bitterness or rebellion. It was his hour of triumph and glory. When the centurion saw how he died, in majestic calm, resigning his spirit into the hands of the Father, he gave glory to God, by saying, in a still small voice: 'Truly this was God's Son.'

Just before Jesus died, he cried out: '*Eli, Eli, lama sabachthani* — not a cry of despair, but the first words of a psalm which expresses perfect trust in God's fidelity. One reason why our Lord used them was perhaps that he wished to give us some words with which to contemplate his cross. We can look to it and say to Jesus, who is God: 'My God, my God, why hast thou left me?' and he himself has provided the answer: 'It is expedient for you that I go, for if I go not, the Holy Spirit will not come.' The Holy Spirit comes upon us when we look at Christ dying on the cross, in perfect conformity to his Father's will, saying: 'Not my will, but thine be done....Father, into thy hands I commend my spirit.' That *is* the Spirit of God's Son, the spirit of sonship, of loving obedience. St Paul had made it his own, through faith, in prayer, and in suffering. It is now our turn to do the same.

Prayer

Almighty and everlasting God our Father, grant that in adversity we may recognize your will and accept it without bitterness, and even with joy, in the Spirit of your Son, our Lord Jesus Christ, who lives and reigns with you in the unity of the same Holy Spirit, and is God, for ever and ever.

12
The Call to Imitate Christ

In the Words of Paul

Let there be one mind in you, the mind of Christ, who, being in the form of God, did not make it his ambition to be treated as God, but emptied himself, and took the form of a servant. He was born in the manner of men, and wearing the appearance of man, he humbled himself, and was obedient unto death, even to death on a cross. Therefore God exalted him greatly, and bestowed on him the name that is above all names, so that in the name of Jesus every knee shall bend, in heaven, on earth, and under the earth, and every tongue shall acclaim Jesus Christ as Lord, to the glory of God his Father.
(Phil 2:5-11)

In the Words of John

They were at supper, and the devil had already put it into the heart of Judas son of Simon, the Iscariot, to play the traitor. Jesus, although he knew that the Father had entrusted all things into his hands, and that he had come from God and was going to God, rose from his place, put aside his clothes, and fastened a towel about his waist. Then he filled a jug with water and made to wash his disciples' feet and wipe them with the towel which he had about him. He came to Simon Peter. But Peter protested: 'Lord, are you going to wash my feet!' Jesus replied: 'You do not now understand what I am doing, but afterwards you will.'...

When he had washed their feet and put on his clothes, he returned to his place and said to them: 'Understand what I have done for you. You call me "Master" and "Lord", and rightly so, for that is what I am. If then I, though Lord and Master, have washed your feet, you too must wash one another's feet. I have set you an example, so that you will do as I have done for you.' (*Jn 13:2-7, 12-15*)

Reflection

In the Washing of Feet, Jesus explicitly calls upon us to imitate him: 'I have set you an example.' But the strange thing here is that he calls upon us to imitate, not his ordinary day-to-day conduct, but something quite exceptional, which he did of set purpose in order to give us a model to imitate. This may seem strange. Surely our daily life ought to imitate his daily life, not something quite exceptional. The Washing of Feet certainly was exceptional, as can be seen from Peter's protest.

The explanation is that the incident was a symbol or an acted parable of the whole ministry of Jesus from his incarnation to his death, and it is this we are called upon to imitate. He rose from the supper table when he left the court of heaven. He stripped himself of his garments, when he laid aside his glory. He girded himself with a towel, when he took our human nature to cleanse us. And he washed our feet when he humbled himself yet further to offer the sacrifice on the cross for the cleansing of our sins.

Seen in this way, the Washing of Feet is very much like this passage from Philippians, where St Paul describes how Christ, being in the form of God, emptied himself of his glory, became a man, and was obedient unto death for our sake. Here too we are explicitly called upon to imitate Christ — to have that mind in us which was in Christ Jesus. But the great advantage of the gospel passage is that it translates into concrete and dramatic terms what is meant by imitating Christ. How can we imitate his self-emptying in his incarnation and in his sacrificial death? By setting no store by our dignity and humbly serving others — by washing their feet, or cleaning their shoes.

There is a similar passage in the First Epistle of St John (3:16-17): 'By this we know love: that he laid down his life for us; and we ought to lay down our *life* for the brethren.' But how can we possibly do that? The next verse gives the answer: 'If anyone has this world's goods and sees his brother in need, yet closes his heart against him, how does the love of God abide in him?' The point is clearer in the Greek original, because the same word (*bios*) means both 'life' and 'livelihood'. As Christ laid down his life for us, so we must lay out our livelihood for the poor.

In the early Church, the liturgy itself must have taught this lesson. In the Eucharistic passage in First Corinthians 11, we see that at Corinth the Eucharist was still celebrated at a common meal. The consecration and breaking of bread was like a solemn grace at the beginning, and the consecration of the cup was a solemn grace at the end. The idea of these common meals (a relic of the sharing of property which was practised at Jerusalem) was that the richer should provide food for the poorer. In connection with such a meal, the Eucharist would have the force of an example: as Christ gives his body to his disciples, so they in their turn must give what is theirs to one another.

The Incarnation was the beginning of a movement of love and reconciliation which is to be continued in and through the Church to the end of time. When Christ said: 'Love one another as I have loved you,' he meant: 'Love one another at some cost to yourselves,' and 'Take the initiative in loving one another, as I took the initiative in coming to you; do not wait for others to make the first move; go out to them with an offer of love and service.' That is how to imitate Christ.

Prayer

Lord Jesus, I believe that you laid down your life for the sake of others, including myself; grant that I may be inspired by your example to spend myself, my talents, and whatever wealth I have, for the good of others. As I daily draw on your wealth in the Eucharist, so may others daily draw upon mine.

13

The Presence of God

The Absence of Paul

So then, my dear friends, just as you have always been obedient in my presence, so now still more in my absence — continue in fear and trembling to work out your salvation. For God is present, working among you, enabling you both to will and to accomplish his good pleasure. Continue without murmuring or disputes. In this way you will be faultless and without defect, innocent children of God in the midst of a crooked and perverse generation. Shine out before them as beacons in the world, offering the word of life. Then I shall be able to boast on the Day of Christ's Judgment that I did not run my course in vain, I did not labour for nothing.
(Phil 2:12-16)

The Absence of Christ

Jesus was at Bethany, in the house of Simon the leper, when a woman came to him with an alabaster flask of costly ointment which she poured over his head while he was at table. The sight of this made the disciples indignant: 'What good is this waste?' they said. 'It

could have been sold for a large sum, and the money given to the poor.' Jesus noticed and said to them: 'Why are you making yourselves unpleasant to the woman? She has done well in doing this for me. The poor you have with you always, but you will not always have me. In pouring this myrrh over my body she has anointed me for burial. I tell you truly, throughout the world, wherever this gospel is preached, the story of what she has done will be told, to honour her memory.'
(*Mt 26:6-13*)

Reflection

St Paul puts on a courageous front by saying that he has good hopes of being released and revisiting Philippi (cf. 1:26), but there are also hints that he knows he may never see the Philippians again and that this letter may be his spiritual testament to them. While writing this passage, he has in mind as his literary model the farewell discourse of Moses to the Israelites at the end of Deuteronomy (31:27): 'Even in my lifetime (Moses says), in spite of my presence among you, you have always been rebelling against the Lord; and when I am gone, worse will follow.' St Paul, by contrast, is able to bear witness that, when he has been present among the Philippians, they have always been obedient to the will of God mediated to them by himself, the Lord's apostle. Like Moses, he fears what may happen when he is gone, but he is less gloomy than Moses, because he believes that God is more powerfully at work in the new covenant than he was in the old (cf. Deut 31:6).

To counteract the effect of his own absence, St Paul reminds the Philippians of two things — of the presence of God, and of the presence of the sinful world.

Remember, he says, that God is at work among you, enabling you both to will and to accomplish his good pleasure. This is true even in the natural order: our every action is supported and made possible by the *concursus* or assistance of God; and it is true again on the supernatural plane: every salutary act, of faith or of any other virtue, is a gift of God in which we cooperate with him. At the beginning of the Epistle, St Paul found in this thought a source of consolation. 'I am confident,' he said, 'that he who began this good work in you will carry it on to completion until the Day of Christ Jesus.' But now he draws from the same thought a warning against any false assurance or slackening of effort; 'Continue in fear and trembling,' he says, 'the work of your salvation, for God is at work among you' — that is, 'Do not vex the divine Spirit within you, and do not spoil his work, but reverence your own person, which God has made his temple.'

We are too familiar with ourselves, and fail to reverence as we should either the divine presence within us, or the dignity which this presence bestows on us — just as the disciples at Bethany had become too familiar with Christ in their midst. They should have been glad when a wealthy woman showed him a special mark of honour and love in reparation for the hostility and contempt of his enemies. Instead, they grumbled at the waste. We are almost as bad, when we forget that Christ is in our midst, when we ignore the divine Spirit whose fragrance fills the whole house, or even drive it away by murmuring and discontent.

The last section of the Epistle exhorted us to humility; this one seems to point in the opposite direction. It reminds us of the presence of God and bids us respect our own dignity as temples of God. 'Recognize, O Christian, your dignity,' says Pope St Leo in a well known sermon. But how can we do this and remain humble at the same time? I suppose, by remembering always that this nature which we reverence in ourselves and in others is a gift of God, who has wonderfully refashioned us by his grace. In practice, we have only to think of our Lady and recite the Magnificat to see how a great saint, the Queen of the saints, combines humility with reverence for her own dignity.

In the second place, St Paul reminds the Philippians of the presence of the world and its corruption. When he looks forward to the Day of Judgment, he sees that he will be responsible for the Philippians. When the Philippians look forward to the Day of Judgment, he would have them remember that they are responsible for the world about them. It is the duty of every Christian community to shine out like a beacon in the world, and to commend the gospel to unbelievers by its own innocence and peace. This too should help Christians to lead a life of virtue: 'I *am* my brother's keeper.'

Prayer

O God, who hast wonderfully created us and still more wonderfully restored us, grant that we may not disfigure your work by unworthy conduct. Make us always sensitive to your presence within us and fearful of wasting the precious talents which you have entrusted to us.

14
Sins of the Tongue

No Murmuring at Philippi!

Continue in fear and trembling to work out your salvation. For God is present, working among you, enabling you both to will and to accomplish his good pleasure. Continue without murmuring or disputes. In this way you will be faultless and without defect, innocent children of God in the midst of a crooked and perverse generation. Shine out before them as beacons in the world, offering the word of life. *(Phil 2:12-16)*

Murmuring at Bethany

Six days before the Pasch, Jesus came to Bethany, the home of Lazarus, whom he had raised from the dead. A supper was given in his honour, at which Martha waited on them, and Lazarus was among those at table with him. Mary brought a pound of costly spikenard ointment and anointed the feet of Jesus and wiped them with her hair, and the house was filled with the fragrance of the ointment. But one of the disciples, Judas Iscariot, the one who was later to betray him, said: 'Why was not this ointment sold for three hundred silver pieces, and the money given to the poor?' (*Jn 12:1-5*)

Reflection

The supper at Bethany is one of the happier incidents in the fourth gospel. Jesus is in the home of a family who *believe* in him. Martha especially makes a great act of faith just before the raising of Lazarus. Jesus says: 'I am the resurrection and the life....Do you believe this?' and Martha replies: 'Yes, Lord, I believe because you are the Christ, the Son of God, the one who was to come into the world.' It is a family which is profoundly *grateful* to him, for raising Lazarus from the dead and restoring him to the family. It is a family that *loves* him and wants to show him a special mark of love and honour.

Christ our Lord appreciated what was done for him. He wanted this incident to be remembered and to be narrated wherever the gospel is preached. It is an example of what every Christian community should be, especially when it meets to celebrate the Eucharist. The liturgy should be a family reunion, of believers, who are *grateful* to Christ (for their spiritual resurrection in baptism), and who want to show him *love* and *honour*. There is an obvious resemblance between Christ's word on this occasion: 'What Mary has done shall be told as a remembrance of her,' and the word which follows the institution of the Eucharist: 'Do this for a commemoration of me.' To borrow a phrase from St Paul, Mary 'discerned the body of the Lord' — she recognized who he was, and treated him with exceptional honour. Unconsciously she set before us a wonderful image of the death of Christ: when she broke the alabaster phial, the fragrance filled the whole house. In the same way, the body of Christ had to be broken on the cross before his Spirit could be poured forth upon the world.

It *should* have been an occasion of great happiness and love and peace. But it was spoiled by the murmuring of Judas — who revealed by what he said his lack of discernment, of belief, of gratitude, of reverence, and of love. He showed no love either for Jesus or for Mary, but presumed to sit in judgment on them both. He lacked the sympathy to enter into Mary's mind and see what she was doing, and why.

There is a warning for us: nothing so quickly ruins the atmosphere of a Christian community, nothing so quickly dispels the gifts of the Spirit, as grumbling and disputes, and harsh words of criticism. In America recently, a young woman told me that before she married, she attended a Catholic university where one of the required courses was on 'Preparation for Marriage'. She said that the priest who gave the lectures went through a long list of harsh and bitter things which a husband and wife must never, never say to each other; and she told me that those lectures had saved her marriage three times over. If we cannot enter sympathetically into the minds of others to see why they are doing what they do, we can at least preserve silence. Silence *is* golden, when it preserves peace.

Prayer

Lord Jesus, Lover of peace, give me the prudence and discretion to control my tongue, lest I spoil the unity and happiness of my companions by murmuring and disputes, or by unkind and unjust criticism. Free me from my past sins of the tongue, and let them be buried in oblivion.

15
The Mystical Body in Action

Servants of Christ

Although my life is being poured out as a libation upon the sacrificial offering of your faith, yet I rejoice for my own sake and for yours; and you too must rejoice both for your own sake and for mine as well.

I hope in the Lord Jesus that I shall be sending Timothy to you soon, so that I may receive some cheering news of how things are with you. I have no one who understands me as he does, and no one who will show such true concern for your well-being. All the rest work for their own interests, not for Christ. But Timothy has proved his worth, as you know. He has worked beside me in the service of the gospel like a son working with his father. So I am hoping to send him to you without further delay, as soon as I can foresee the outcome of my case; and I am confident that I shall be coming myself before long.

Meanwhile, I think it advisable to send back to you

Epaphroditus, my brother, the sharer of my labours and battles, and your messenger, sent to minister to my needs. He has been homesick for you all and upset because you had heard that he was ill. He was indeed ill, and nearly died; but God had mercy on him — and not on him alone, but on me as well, or there would have been a fresh grief added to my others. So I am sending him to you sooner than I would have done, so that you will have the joy of seeing him again, and I shall be free of anxiety. Give him a truly joyful and Christian welcome.

You must hold in honour a man like this, who came near to death in Christ's service, and risked his life to do for me the one remaining thing which you had not been able to do in my service. *(Phil 2:17-30)*

God's Harvesters

A possessed man who was deaf and dumb was brought to Jesus. After the devil had been expelled, the dumb man spoke. The people were filled with wonder and said: 'Nothing like this has ever appeared in Israel!' But the Pharisees said: 'It is by the power of the prince of devils that he expels devils.'

As Jesus went round all the towns and villages, proclaiming the good news of the kingdom and curing every disease and every illness, his heart was touched with pity for the people whom he saw, for they were harassed and worried, like shepherdless sheep.

Then he said to his disciples: 'The harvest is abundant, but the labourers are few; pray, therefore, to the Lord of the harvest, that he will send labourers to reap his harvest.' *(Mt 9:32-37)*

Reflection

Although this section of the Epistle is concerned with practical matters — the comings and goings of St Paul's helpers — it also embodies some valuable points of instruction.

Paul is sending Timothy to look after the spiritual welfare of the Philippians, to teach and preach among them, and to keep Paul informed of what is going on. He is also sending back Epaphroditus, whom the Philippians had sent to take care of the material welfare of Paul in prison. While looking after Paul, he had fallen ill and started worrying because the people at home were worrying about him. So Paul has reluctantly decided to send him back. He assures the people of Philippi that Epaphroditus has not failed in his charge. On the contrary, he has fulfilled his office well, and they must receive him back with joy and honour.

From all this, one thing is plain: these early Christians did love one another. They were not hard-hearted and detached individualists; they felt for one another, shared one another's joys and sorrows, missed one another, wanted news of one another, and what one could not do, the others did for him. Here we see the doctrine of the Mystical Body in action. St Paul never uses the high-flown term 'Mystical Body', but he does compare the Church as a whole, and each individual community, to a body: each part lives for the good of the whole; if any part suffers, the other parts suffer in sympathy; if any member is filled with joy, all share this joy; not every member has the same function, but each fulfils his own role for the good of the whole. If it is now Paul's role to suffer imprisonment, and even to pour out his life for the sake of the Church, to defend its faith, he accepts this with joy, and calls on the Philippians to share his joy.

A less high-flown way of expressing the doctrine of the Mystical Body is to say that God does not deal with us as isolated individuals. Pope Pius XII once said: 'It is a great mystery, on which we do not meditate enough, that God has made the salvation of one man dependent on the actions of another' — for better or for worse. If the Pharisees had not opposed our Lord, a much larger part of Israel might have been converted. If St Paul had not exerted himself as a missionary, the church of Philippi might not have been founded at all. As he said earlier in the Epistle, 'God is at work in us.' But God does not force our hand: it rests with us either to carry out the work which he wills to do through us, or to be lazy and do nothing, or even to turn round and work against him. The history of the Church has not followed an inevitable course through the centuries. If men had cooperated better, the Church would be larger, holier, more united; if they had cooperated less well, it would be weaker, poorer, and even more divided.

These ideas are also expressed in the passage from the end of Matthew 9. When our Lord travelled up and down the land, and saw the spiritual condition of the people, 'his entrails were upset.' That is what the Greek says; in more idiomatic English we can say: 'his heart was touched with pity for them.'[1] And he said to his disciples: 'Pray to the Lord of the harvest that he will send reapers.' The harvest will not be reaped unless God sends the reapers; and in his providence he has so disposed that reapers will not be sent unless we pray for them. So God has made the salvation of our fellow men dependent on our prayers and efforts to spread the gospel. What are we going to do about it?

A young African Jesuit recently began his sermon in a parish church in Oxford by saying: 'At the age of ten, I was apprenticed to a witch-doctor; it is thanks to

---

[1] See above, p. 20.

your generosity and prayers that I am now a Christian and a priest.'

Prayer

O Lord of the harvest, send labourers into your fields. If we are worthy, send us; and if we are not worthy, even so send us, so that your strength may be manifested through our weakness. Breathe into our hearts the gentleness and compassion which filled the heart of our Saviour. Grant that we may understand the gospel and proclaim to the men of our generation the words of life for which they hunger.

16

The Chain of Tradition

Formation by Imitation

Although my life is being poured out as a libation upon the sacrificial offering of your faith, yet I rejoice for my own sake and for yours; and you too must rejoice both for your own sake and for mine as well.

I hope in the Lord Jesus that I shall be sending Timothy to you soon, so that I may receive some cheering news of how things are with you. I have no one who understands me as he does, and no one who will show such true concern for your well-being. All the rest work for their own interests, not for Christ. But Timothy has proved his worth, as you know. He has worked beside me in the service of the gospel like a son working with his father. So I am hoping to send him to you without further delay, as soon as I can foresee the outcome of my case; and I am confident that I shall be coming myself before long. *(Phil 2:17-24)*

Unchristian Leadership

Since the scribes and Pharisees have occupied the chair of Moses, you must heed and do all that they say to you, but do not imitate what they do, for they do not obey their own teaching. They bind heavy and unbearable burdens and pile them on other men's shoulders, but themselves never stir a finger to move them.

All that they do is done to be seen by men: they widen their phylacteries and broaden the hems of their cloaks; they love to have places of honour at banquets and the first seats in the synagogues, to be bowed to in the market-places, and addressed by the people as 'Rabbi'. But you must not take the title of 'Rabbi'; there is one master over you, and you are all brothers. And do not address anyone on earth as your 'Father'; there is only one Father for you, your Father in heaven. And do not take the title of 'Teacher'; you must have only one Teacher, Christ.

The greatest among you must be your servant. Whoever exalts himself will be humbled, and whoever humbles himself will be exalted. (*Mt 23:1-12*)

Reflection

In the passage from Matthew 23, Jesus attacks the Pharisees because they do not practise what they preach; they teach by precept only, not by example. They take honorific titles, and regard themselves as being above the law which they impose on others. The disciples of Christ are to be far different: they are not to give themselves high-sounding titles, and they must teach in the first place by their example.

In Philippians, St Paul describes himself and Timothy simply as 'servants of Christ Jesus' (1:1), and addresses the officials of the church by the very modest titles of 'supervisors' (*episkopoi*[1]) *and* 'servants' (*diakonoi*). His and their office is to teach Christian behaviour chiefly by example. When he talks about 'traditions', he usually means, not doctrinal traditions, but patterns of behaviour. He calls upon the Philippians to imitate Christ who emptied himself and became a man and a servant of men. Later, he points out that he himself has imitated the self-emptying of Christ in rejecting as refuse all that was his glory, in order to become the servant of others — and he calls upon the Philippians to imitate himself too. In this present passage, he describes Timothy as being 'of like soul' with himself — he has been formed in the image of Paul by watching him as a son watches his father and learns his ways (cf. Jn 5:18-20). As Paul's life is almost spent (2:17), Timothy must take over his work.[2] The Philippians must imitate him too — and all others who follow the pattern of conduct transmitted to them by Paul (cf. 3:17). There is a chain of tradition within the New Testament: from the Father to Christ, from Christ to Paul, from Paul to Timothy, from Timothy to the Philippians.

A chain of tradition should run through the life of every Christian community. Its 'leaders' (Heb 13:7, 17, 24) should set a pattern for others to imitate. Since Vatican II, there has been much uncertainty in religious orders and congregations as to what they should call their leaders. The word 'superior' is frowned upon as being unevangelical. It would be hard to improve upon the ancient title 'abbot', for this means 'father' and suggests that monks and religious should imitate their

---

[1] *Episkopos* is the regular Greek word for a 'bishop'. Etymologically, it means an 'overseer'. In the New Testament, it is still synonymous with the word 'presbyter' (cf. Acts 20:17,28).

[2] The structure of the prologue of the Epistle (1:1-2) suggests that as Timothy will take over from Paul, so the deacons will one day take over from the presbyter-bishops.

leader as Timothy imitated Paul. In every Christian community — monastery, school, convent, hospital, parish, diocese — it is the duty of the leaders to represent Christ, by living in the Spirit of Christ, and setting an example of Christlike conduct.

Prayer

Raise up among us, O heavenly Father, leaders who will reflect the fidelity and compassion of your Son; and give us all the humility to learn from their example.

17

How not to Imitate Christ

Judaism Obsolete

For the rest, my brethren, rejoice in the Lord. To keep repeating the same advice 'causes me no apprehension, and to you no peril brings'.[1] Beware of dogs, beware of malefactors, beware of mutilation of the flesh. It is we who are the true circumcision — we who worship in the Spirit of God, who place our trust in Christ Jesus, and put no confidence in the flesh. And yet I have grounds for confidence in the flesh — indeed if anyone has, I have still more: circumcised on my eighth day, an Israelite by birth, of the tribe of Benjamin, Hebrew-speaking and of Hebrew-speaking parents; in regard to the law a Pharisee; as for my zeal, I persecuted the Church; as for the justice that comes from the law, there was nothing wrong with me. But all those things that were to my credit, for Christ's sake I now consider

---

[1] In the Greek, this phrase is an iambic trimeter. It seems to be a quotation.

liabilities. In fact there is now nothing I do not regard as such, so far does the privilege of knowing Christ Jesus my Lord surpass all other advantages. For his sake I have forfeited all those things. I count them as refuse, in order to win Christ, to be in him, and to possess, not a justice of my own making based on the law, but the justice that comes through faith in Christ, God's justice, based on faith. (*Phil 3:1-9*)

Salvation for Gentiles

When Jesus came down from the mountain, large crowds followed him. A leper came and knelt before him and said: 'Lord, if it is your will, you can make me clean.' Jesus stretched out his hand and touched him: 'It is my will,' he said, 'be made clean!' And at once the man's leprosy was cleansed. Then Jesus said to him: 'See that you tell no one, but go and show yourself to the priest, and offer the gift which Moses laid down, for a witness to them.'

He went into Capharnaum, and a centurion came to him with this entreaty: 'Lord,' he said, 'my boy is stricken down at home with paralysis, and is in great pain.' Jesus said to him: 'I will come and cure him.' But the centurion replied: 'Lord, I am not worthy that you should enter under my roof. I know that you have only to say a word, and my boy will be cured; for I too am a man with authority. I have soldiers under me: I say to this one "Go", and he goes, and to another "Come", and he comes, and to my slave "Do this" and he does it.' When Jesus heard this, he was amazed and said to his followers: 'I tell you truly, I have not found such faith in Israel! I tell you, many will come from east and west, and take their places with Abraham and Isaac and Jacob in the kingdom of heaven; but the heirs of the kingdom will be thrown outside, where there will be weeping and gnashing of teeth!' Then he said to the centurion: 'Go! As you have believed, so be it done for you.' And the boy was cured at that very hour.

(*Mt 8:1-13*)

Reflection

In the last section of the Epistle, St Paul announced that he was sending Timothy to take care of the spiritual welfare of the Philippians. In this one, he makes it fairly clear what he is afraid of, and why he thinks the Philippians need Timothy to teach and preach among them.

Whenever St Paul founded a church among the Gentiles, he told his converts to remain Gentiles — not to have themselves circumcised, and not to adopt the Jewish way of life, but to stay as they were, Gentiles. Then he would move on to work elsewhere, and there would follow in his path certain Jewish teachers who told his converts that Paul had misled them, and that if they wanted to be saved, they must 'judaize', that is, they must adopt the Jewish way of life by submitting to circumcision and the law of Moses (cf. Acts 15:5). These 'judaizing teachers' (as they are often called) had some powerful arguments: they could say: 'Christ himself was circumcised and obeyed the law, and he said that not one jot or tittle of it would pass away — he had not come to abolish it. He did not say, as Paul says, that the law is obsolete.' These men were doubtless in good faith. But St Paul deals roughly with them. 'Beware of the dogs!' he says, with only the slightest trace of humour to soften the words.

From the present section of the Epistle we gather that he is afraid the Philippians may be bitten by these dogs, that is, they may succumb to the judaizing propaganda and lose their faith in the gospel as he preached it.

So he is going to send Timothy to defend the gospel as he preached it, and meanwhile he sends this letter, saying: 'Look at me! I was about as perfect a Jew as it is possible to be: a thoroughbred of the tribe of Benjamin, circumcised on my eighth day, a Hebrew-speaker since childhood, brought up as a Pharisee, so zealous for the law that I actually persecuted the Church. And what good did all that do to me? None at all! I have rejected the whole thing as so much rubbish or refuse, in order to put my faith in Christ. And now I am warning you that Judaism will not do you any good either. On the contrary, it will do you much harm. So beware of these dogs, these malefactors, these mutilators of the flesh!' Now: *was Paul right?*

In the first of the miracle-stories from Matthew 8, our Lord, by sending the cured leper to the priest at the temple, to offer the sacrifice laid down in the law, shows his reverence for the temple, the priesthood, the sacrifices, and the law of Moses. Is it possible, then, that Paul was wrong in rejecting all these things? If a Christian is to imitate Christ, should he not imitate Christ's observance of the law? The answer is that Paul was not wrong. Jesus said: 'Not a jot or tittle of the law shall pass away until the whole is fulfilled.' On the cross he cried: 'It is fulfilled, *Consummatum est!* and died, and at once the veil of the temple was rent from top to bottom. His death marked the end of the temple, the animal sacrifices, the priesthood, and the old law.

In the second miracle-story, Jesus sees the faith of the Gentile centurion (an officer in the Roman army) as a portent of the growth of the Gentile churches, made up of men and women who would be cured by faith in his power and authority (not by the law of Moses): 'Many will come from east and west...' Immediately after his death, on Calvary itself, it is a Gentile centurion who says: 'Truly this was God's Son!'

St Paul had understood the mind of Christ, and was carrying on the work of Christ. He understood that circumcision and the ceremonial law belonged to a primitive stage of religion which had been rendered obsolete by the death of Christ. It was time to forget the past and look to the future — to serve God, not with the sacrifice of animals, but by the spiritual sacrifice of faith working through charity, by pouring out one's life in the service of other people (cf. 2:17).

Jesus himself announced that a new era was about to commence in which the old religious rituals would have no place (Jn 4:23): 'The hour is coming, and is already here, when true worshippers will worship the Father in spirit and truth' — no longer with the flesh of animals but with spiritual sacrifices, and no longer with symbolic rites but with true worship.

St Paul understood that Christ became subject to the law, not in order to set a model of strict observance, but in order to liberate his fellow Jews from the law (cf. Gal 4:4-5). Therefore to imitate Christ intelligently we must not imitate his observance of the law of Moses. We are called upon to follow the example of his self-emptying, his obedience, and his humble service of others. That is what St Paul has done in abandoning the Judaism which was once his pride; and that is what the Philippians must do in their turn and according to their circumstances.

Prayer

O God our Father, who called us to worship you in spirit and truth, may our lives be poured out in the service of our neighbour; may our faith and charity go up like the smoke of incense, an odour of sweetness, acceptable to your divine majesty. Through our Lord Jesus Christ your Son, who lives and reigns with you in the unity of the Holy Spirit, God, for ever and ever.

18

Imitating the Samaritan

Non-Jewish Justice

All those things that were to my credit, for Christ's sake I now consider liabilities. In fact there is now nothing I do not regard as such, so far does the privilege of knowing Christ Jesus my Lord surpass all other advantages. For his sake I have forfeited all those things. I count them as refuse, in order to win Christ, to be in him, and to possess, not a justice of my own making based on the law, but the justice that comes through faith in Christ, God's justice, based on faith, so that I may know him and experience the power of his resurrection. *(Phil 3:7-10)*

Non-Jewish Charity

Once a lawyer rose and put a question to test Jesus. 'Master,' he asked, 'what must I do to gain eternal life?'

Jesus replied: 'In the law what is written? What do you read there?' He answered: 'Love the Lord your God with your whole heart, and with your whole soul, and with your whole strength, and with your whole mind, and your neighbour as yourself.' Jesus said to him: 'You have answered rightly; do this and you will have life.'

The lawyer, however, wishing to justify himself, said to Jesus: 'But who is my "neighbour"?' Jesus gave him this answer. 'A man was on his way down from Jerusalem to Jericho when he fell into the hand of robbers, who stripped him and beat him, and went away leaving him half dead. A priest happened to be going down that way; he saw him and passed by. A levite too came along the road; he saw him and passed by. But a Samaritan on his travels came upon him, and when he saw him, his heart was touched with pity. He went over to him, treated his wounds with oil and wine and bound them up, then put him astride his own mount and brought him to an inn, and took care of him. Next day, he took out two silver pieces and gave them to the inn-keeper. "Look after him," he said, "and anything that you spend over and above this, I will repay you when I come back." Now, which of these three, do you think, proved himself a neighbour to the man who fell into the hands of the robbers?' He said: 'The one who showed him charity.' Jesus replied: 'Go and do as he did.' (*Lk 10:25-37*)

Reflection

In this brief section of the Epistle, St Paul draws a contrast between seeking justice from the law of Moses and seeking justice from faith in Christ. By 'seeking justice' or 'seeking righteousness', he means seeking to enter into a right relationship with God. He contrasts two ways of doing this: the way of the law, and the way of faith in Christ.

He himself had tried both. Before his conversion, he applied himself to the study and observance of the law, until by his own standards he was perfect; if anyone in Jerusalem was a just man by Paul's standard, it was Paul — and he was looked up to and honoured by others as a zealous Pharisee. But by means of the vision on the road to Damascus he was taught that this 'justice' on which he prided himself made him a just man only in human eyes, not in the eyes of God. Far from serving the Lord, he was persecuting the Lord in his members: 'Saul, Saul, why are you persecuting me?' Through this experience, he was shown that the way to become a just man, the way to enter into a right relationship with God, was *not* to be a strict observer of the law, but to be one of those despised disciples of Jesus — to believe in him and be accepted by him into that almost-identification which is implied in 'Why are you persecuting *me*?'

Before his conversion, St Paul believed that 'justice' was a personal achievement, to be attained by careful study of the law and rigorous self-discipline. His conversion experience taught him that if there is to be a right relation between God and sinful man, God must take the initiative — as he has done in Christ — and all we are required to do is to accept his forgiveness as a free gift, granted to us through the merits of Christ's cross. This we do by recognizing the truth — by believing that the cross is what it is, the sacrifice of our redemption. Through this faith we enter into a right relationship with God in Christ based on truth. He forgives us, and takes possession of us through our faith.

So St Paul had experienced two quite different kinds of religion: the religion of personal effort, self-improvement, self-assertion, and self-admiration; and the religion of humble acceptance and surrender. He says that the one is rubbish by comparison with the other. By our own unaided efforts we are not likely to achieve anything except pharisaic pride; but the man who comes to know Christ is transformed by this knowledge.

When St Paul talks about 'knowing' Christ, he means more than simply knowing his name. To 'know' a person is to get to know his mind and his character, to feel the influence of his thought and his will. From the day of his conversion, St Paul 'knew' Christ — knew him as a person of surpassing power and goodness. To enter into union with him through faith is to come within a new sphere of power, to be lifted out of one's old mediocre self and made capable of serving God in charity, joy and peace.

It was with a great sigh of relief that Paul abandoned the way of the law and committed himself to the way of faith in Christ. He did so wholeheartedly. When Christ sent him to the Gentiles, he went to the Gentiles, he entered Gentile houses, and ate with Gentiles — things which the law forbade; and he abandoned the Jewish calendar with its feasts and fasts. In the eyes of the law-observing Jews, Paul was now a sinner and a renegade; but he was not distressed about that, because he knew that in God's eyes he was now a just man, thanks to Christ our Lord.

However, as was mentioned above, there were even Christian Jews who thought that St Paul was wrong, and that he *was* a sinner for abandoning the law — because, they thought, Christ had endorsed the law. The passage from Luke 10 again helps us to see that Paul had understood the mind of Christ better than they had.

The opening exchange of the dialogue is not too promising. The lawyer asks the important question: 'What must I do to gain eternal life?' and Christ immediately refers him to the law: 'In the law what is written? How do you read?' It looks as though he is going to endorse the law of Moses. But when he comes on to the parable, we learn that if ever the precepts of the ceremonial law come into conflict with the precepts of charity, the ceremonial law must yield: the priest and the levite, exponents of the ritual law, fail to fulfil the law of charity. They pass by unmoved, fearing to incur a ritual defilement by touching what looks like a corpse. But the Samaritan, who is not impeded by any ceremonial law, sees the wounded man, his heart is touched with pity, and he cares for the man.

Our Lord is saying, by this parable, that the ritual law can become an impediment to works of charity, and then it must be abandoned. In the parable it impedes a corporal work of mercy; in the apostolic Church it was impeding spiritual works of mercy: apostles and missionaries were reluctant to go and teach the Gentiles, for fear of breaking the law — until St Paul understood that this was not Christ's intention; Christ meant them to go to the Gentiles in spite of the law. So he courageously abandoned the law and became the servant of Christ, seeking justification not from the law but from faith in Christ.

The lesson for us is that if we are going to respond to our vocation as Paul did to his — if we are going to do what God wants us to do in this world, we must not put much faith in any particular practices or devotions of our own choosing, but must surrender and put ourselves at the disposal of Christ. This should not be too difficult to do if our life of prayer centres round the Eucharist. In the Eucharist we surrender our person to the will of Christ. He comes in, and we are in his power, to change us as he wills, so that he can use us as instruments of his charity and mercy among our fellow men. That is why it is good to say after Communion the prayer of St Ignatius: 'Take, O Lord, and receive all my liberty, my memory, understanding and will — take my powers and use them.'

Prayer

O God, the Giver of life, enlighten our minds to understand the weakness of our fallen nature and the strength of our Risen Lord; grant that through faith in him we may produce the fruits of righteousness.

A Note on St Augustine's Interpretation of the Good Samaritan.

St Augustine's allegorical interpretation of the Good Samaritan is nowadays quoted as an example of how *not* to interpret the parables. He says:

> *A certain man went down from Jerusalem to Jericho:* Adam himself is meant; *Jerusalem* is the heavenly city of peace, from whose blessedness Adam fell: *Jericho* means the moon, and signifies our mortality, because it is born, waxes, wanes, and dies. *Thieves* are the devil and his angels. *Who stripped him,* namely, of his immortality; *and beat him,* by persuading him to sin; *and left him half-dead,* because in so far as man can understand and know God, he lives, but in so far as he is wasted and oppressed by sin, he is dead; he is therefore called *half-dead.* The *priest* and the *levite* who saw him and passed by, signify the priesthood and ministry of the Old Testament, which could profit nothing for salvation. *Samaritan* means Guardian, and therefore the Lord himself is signified by this name. The *binding of the wounds* is the restraint of sin . . .

Professor Dodd's comment is: 'To the ordinary person of intelligence who approaches the Gospels with some sense for literature this mystification must appear quite perverse.'[1] However, St Augustine himself was not without some sense of literature.

The parable presents a problem similar to the one discussed above in connection with the Washing of Feet:

---
[1] C.H. Dodd, *The Parables of the Kingdom*, London,, 1936, p. 13.

If we are to imitate Christ, should we not imitate his daily conduct rather than something exceptional which he did once (the Washing of Feet) or a story which he made up (the Good Samaritan)? The answer is much the same in both cases.[1] St Augustine was right in recognizing that the story of the Good Samaritan is an allegorical description of Christ's ministry. Undoubtedly Augustine decodes too many details, but one has only to ask whether Christ himself obeyed the teaching embodied in this parable, and it springs to mind at once that this is exactly what he was doing all the time. Mankind had been weakened and wounded by sin, and was in a helpless condition. The priesthood of the old covenant had proved ineffectual, as the Epistle to the Hebrews says (7:19, etc.). Christ came to heal mankind. He poured in oil and wine, representing the grace of the sacraments and perhaps the material rites as well. He himself paid the cost of the cure; and when the injured man awoke to what had happened, Christ was gone, but will return.

If the parable is an allegorical description of Christ's ministry, we have only to imitate the Good Samaritan, and we are thereby imitating Christ.

---

[1] On the Washing of Feet, see above, p. 55.

19

Dying with Christ

Paul dies with Christ

All those things that were to my credit, for Christ's sake I now consider liabilities. In fact there is now nothing I do not regard as such, so far does the privilege of knowing Christ Jesus my Lord surpass all other advantages. For his sake I have forfeited all those things. I count them as refuse, in order to win Christ, to be in him, and to possess, not a justice of my own making based on the law, but the justice that comes through faith in Christ, God's justice, based on faith, so that I may know him and experience the power of his resurrection and fellowship in his sufferings. I become like him in his death, in the hope of attaining the resurrection from the dead. *(Phil 3:7-11)*

The Good Thief dies with Christ

Two others were led out with him, criminals to be put to death. When they came to the place called Calvary, they crucified him there, with the criminals one on his right and one on his left.

One of the criminals jeered at him: 'Are you not the Messiah?' he said. 'Then if you are, save yourself — and us!' But the other criminal broke in and rebuked him: 'Do you not even fear God, when you are under the same sentence? Our sentence at least is just; we are only getting what our crimes deserved; but this man has done nothing wrong.' Then he said: 'Jesus, remember me when you come with your royal power!' Jesus replied: 'I tell you truly, this very day you shall be with me in paradise.'
(*Lk 23:32-33, 38-43*)

Reflection

The Gospel according to St Luke is traditionally associated with the preaching of St Paul. On the whole, its contents are not particularly Pauline. There are, however, two passages given by St Luke alone, which contain the characteristic doctrine of St Paul that a man is justified by faith and not by works.

The first is the parable of the Pharisee and the Publican (18: 10-14). The Pharisee goes into the temple and boasts of his good works; the publican stands afar off, beats his breast, and asks for mercy: 'Lord, have mercy on me a sinner!' And, Jesus says, it was the publican who went home justified (or forgiven), not the Pharisee.

The other passage is the one given above, the story of the two 'thieves' on Calvary. Here too we have a contrast. The first thief actually prays for salvation: 'Save yourself,' he says, '*and us!*' But he prays without faith or hope or charity, and his mocking prayer is ignored. He was crucified with Christ, and in this sense 'became like him in his death', but he blasphemed Christ on the cross, and who knows the fate of his soul? The second thief took Christ's side, by rebuking the first.

Then he made an honest confession of his guilt: 'Our sentence is at least just; we are only getting what our sins deserve.' Then he declares Jesus innocent: 'But this man has done nothing wrong!' How that must have touched the heart of Christ, the sympathy of his fellow-sufferer! Then through some great gift of grace, the man made an heroic act of faith: 'Jesus, remember me when you come in your royal power!' The cross, he believes, cannot be the end; the title proclaims Jesus king, and he *will* come in glory, in spite of the cross! In reply Jesus grants him a complete pardon for his sins: 'This day you will be with me in paradise.' There is the answer to his faith, hope and charity!

In this tableau on Calvary, we see on the one side faith, justification, forgiveness, hope; on the other side disbelief, hatred and despair. In the middle, Jesus is lifted up, that whosoever believes in him may not perish but may have eternal life.

Justification, salvation, reconciliation, forgiveness, these words are near-synonyms for the gift of grace offered to all men on the same terms: if we believe that Christ is who he is, the Son of God, and unite ourselves through faith with his death, the sacrifice of expiation for our sins. Observance of Jewish rituals is not necessary — salvation is not offered to Jews alone, but to all men of every race and nation.

There are two symbols of the universality of the gospel in the narrative of the crucifixion. First, St Mark says that Simon of Cyrene was the father of Alexander and Rufus. To explain this detail, it is often said that Alexander and Rufus must have been personally known to the evangelist. Perhaps they were. But is it a coincidence that the three names are 'Simon', which is Hebrew, 'Alexandros', which is Greek, and 'Rufus', which is Latin? Secondly, all three languages were used for the title on the cross, to proclaim to the whole world that Jesus was king. Perhaps the evangelist saw in these details a sign of the fulfilment of the vision of Daniel 7, where the Son of Man is given dominion over all 'peoples, nations and languages.' At all events, in the fourth gospel, we are told that 'God gave his only Son, that whosoever believes in him may have eternal life' (3:16); and the Samaritans recognize him as 'the Saviour of the world' (4:42).

Prayer

O Lord God our Father, who hast given us in the cross of your Son a perfect sacrifice of reconciliation, unite all men of every people, nation and language in the one faith, so that we may live in peace and charity, according to your will. Father of all, thy kingdom come!

20
Assimilation to Christ Crucified

Paul Dead and Risen

I have forfeited all those things....so that I may know Christ and experience the power of his resurrection and fellowship in his sufferings. I become like him in his death, in the hope of attaining the resurrection from the dead. *(Phil 3:9-11)*

The Lamb that was slain

While they were still talking about all this, Jesus stood in the middle of them and said: 'Peace be upon you!' But panic and fear seized them, for they thought they were seeing a ghost. Jesus said to them: 'Why this confusion? Why do these doubts spring up in your hearts? Look at my hands and my feet, and see that it is myself! Touch me and see: a ghost has no flesh or bones as you see that I have.' With this, he showed them his hands and feet. Then, as they were so overjoyed and astonished that they still could not bring themselves to believe it, he said to them: 'Have you anything here to eat?' They gave him a piece of roasted fish, which he took and ate before their eyes.

Then he said to them: 'This is what I meant when I said to you while I was still with you that everything written about me in the law of Moses and in the prophets and the psalms must be fulfilled.' Then he opened their minds to understand the Scriptures. 'This,' he said, 'is what the Scriptures say: the Messiah must suffer, but three days later he will rise from the dead, and in his name repentance for the forgiveness of sins is to be proclaimed to all the nations, beginning from Jerusalem.'
(Lk 24:36-47)

Reflection

The first appearance of the Lord to the disciples in Jerusalem after his resurrection is, in a way, complementary to the trial before Caiphas just before his death. In each scene the question is: Who is Jesus? Caiphas and his assistants would not believe that Jesus was the Son of God; the disciples in the upper room found it hard to believe that he was a real man. As at the Walking on the Water, they feared that he might be a ghost. But this time, they hesitated to believe through sheer joy. St Luke probably means that they were reluctant to say 'Yes, it *is* the Lord' for fear of the disappointment which would follow, if it turned out that they were mistaken.

To convince them, Jesus ate a piece of fish in their presence. When he had left them, if they wondered whether it had been a collective hallucination, there were the remains of the fish on the plate.

He also showed them his hands and side, as he was to show them to Thomas a week later: they were to feel his flesh and bones and see the marks of the nails. This was the very same crucified body that had vanished from the tomb; it was now filled with indestructible life, but it was the same body.

So the answer to the question, Who is this? was: 'Christ crucified.' That is a permanent title of Christ. He remains for ever Christ crucified, or, in the language of the Apocalypse, the Lamb that was slain. In a sense, his death is a part of his life, and lives on in his glory. Just as we ourselves can never shake off our past, but have to live with it because it has made us what we are, so too with Christ: he lives on as one who has experienced our life and our death and has passed on beyond. According to the Epistle to the Hebrews, this is what makes him the perfect High Priest. Having shared our life and death, he has compassion for us; and having been obedient unto death, he has attained a degree of fidelity to his Father which could not be attained except through great suffering.

Just as the risen Christ remains Christ crucified, so we, who wish to imitate him, must constantly die with him to this world, in order to experience the power of his resurrection. Death and resurrection go together: death is the denial of our earthly life, and resurrection is the negation of this death. That is why one can share in the powers of the world to come only by sharing in the cross. Each disciple must translate this principle into concrete terms for himself. We hear much about self-fulfilment these days. The Christian paradox is that self-fulfilment comes about by self-emptying.

Prayer

Give us the courage, O heavenly Father, to take up our cross and follow Jesus Christ your Son, so that we too may know him and experience the power of his resurrection, without which we can do nothing.

21
Paul in Pursuit of Perfection

The Race for Perfection

I do not say that I have already won the prize or reached perfection, but I am pressing on to take hold of it — or rather, Christ has taken hold of me. Brethren, I do not consider myself to have won the prize already; but one thing I claim: I forget about what is behind and strain towards what is ahead, and press on to the finishing line to win the prize of the high vocation to which God has called me in Christ Jesus. So then, let us view our lives in this way, those of us who are perfect; if you have taken any other view, God will reveal the truth of this one to you in time. Only let us persevere in the course we are now pursuing. *(Phil 3:12-16)*

The Price of Perfection

A man came to Jesus and said: 'Master, what good work must I do to win everlasting life?' Jesus said to him: 'Why do you question me about the good? There is one alone who is good. But if you desire to enter life, keep the commandments.' He asked: 'Which commandments do you mean?' Jesus said: 'You shall not kill, you shall not commit adultery, you shall not steal, you shall not bear false witness, honour your father and your mother, and love your neighbour as yourself." The young man answered: 'I have kept all these commandments; what else must I do?' Jesus replied: 'If you wish to be perfect, go and sell your property and give the money to the poor — and you will have treasure in heaven — then come back and follow me.' When the young man heard this answer, he turned sadly away, for he owned great wealth. *(Mt 19:16-22)*

Reflection

Before St Paul was converted, he imagined that he had already attained perfection. Already he was the perfect Jew; in regard to the justice that comes from the law, he was faultless. In the crisis of conversion, he was taught, like the rich young man, that if he wanted to be perfect, he must cast aside every worldly advantage upon which he might pride himself, and follow Christ along the road that leads to Calvary. Another of the paradoxes of Christianity is that for a true disciple, 'perfection' consists in recognizing that in this life one is never perfect. The only perfection we can attain in this life is constant movement towards a goal which is never reached in this life.

The Greek word for 'perfect' can also mean 'adult' or 'mature' (cf. 1 Cor 14:20). St Paul is therefore saying that for a Christian there is no end-state in this world, which a man can achieve at the age of thirty-five or so, and after which he is 'mature' or 'perfect'. The whole of this life is an effort *towards* an end-state which is reached only after death. St Paul claims to have imitated the self-emptying of Christ, but he is well aware that his self-emptying falls far short of the perfection of Christ's obedience and humility.

He regards the Christian vocation as an invitation to run a race and seek a prize. The imagery is not in all respects appropriate: the runners in this race do not compete against one another, and all who run well receive the prize. But in other respects, it can be useful. A well trained runner does not look backwards to see how much ground he has already covered, or to find in the slackness of others an excuse for slackening his own effort. He keeps his eyes on what is ahead, namely, the tape and the pace-setters in front of him. But what St Paul means in particular is that he deliberately 'forgets' (by putting out of mind) his previous claims to privilege, his previous standards of judgment, his previous ambitions, and his Pharisaic habit of self-congratulation, in order to follow Christ who has run far ahead — not that he is able to follow by his own strength, but Christ has taken hold of him.

'I forget what is behind and strain towards what is ahead' is a particularly fitting motto for Christians of the present day. The process of renewal initiated by Pope John XXIII requires us to abandon many old customs and accept new ways of thinking and acting. One point which we must all settle with ourselves is this: that at the behest of Christ's Holy Spirit working in his Church we will forget what is behind and stretch out to what lies ahead. The reunion of the churches, for example, will never come about, if we nurse old grievances and cling to obsolete traditions.

Prayer

Renew in us, Lord Jesus, the strength and resolution to follow you steadfastly and unswervingly day by day, as we press on to receive the promised prize. Rid us of the pride and selfishness which prevent us from doing perfectly the will of our Father in heaven.

22
Citizens of a Better World

Look Upwards!

Brethren, unite in following my example, and keep your eyes on those who live according to the model which my own conduct set before you. There are many who go a far different way. I have often told you before, and now I tell you with tears: they are enemies of the cross of Christ, and their end will be utter ruin. Their god is their belly; they glory in their shame; their hearts are bent on earthly things. But as for us, our citizenship is in heaven; it is to heaven that we look expectantly for the Coming of Jesus Christ as our Saviour. He will transform our bodies from their present humble state into the likeness of the body which he has in his glory. For he has power to make all things subject to himself. So then, my dear and much loved brethren, my joy and my crown, persevere as you are in the Lord, my beloved.

(Phil 3:17—4:1)

Truth passes Understanding

Some Pharisees and some of Herod's courtiers were then sent to Jesus to ensnare him in an argument. They came and said to him: 'Master, we know that you speak the truth and are afraid of no one; you are not swayed by human respect, but teach the way of God as it truly is. Now, is it lawful to pay taxes to Caesar or not? Are we to pay them, or are we not?' Jesus saw their duplicity and said to them: 'Why do you try to trap me? Show me a silver coin.' They produced one; and he said to them: 'Whose is this image and inscription?' 'Caesar's,' they replied. Jesus said to them: 'Render to Caesar the things that are Caesar's, and to God the things that are God's!' — an answer which took them by surprise.

Then he was approached by some of the Sadducees (men who maintain that there is no resurrection); and the question they put to him was this: 'Master, Moses laid down a law for us that a man whose brother dies and leaves a widow but no child, must himself marry the widow and beget children for his brother. Take the case of seven brothers: the first married a wife, and died without issue. So the second married her, and he too died leaving no children. So also did the third. In fact the seven of them left no children. Finally the woman died. Now, at the resurrection, when they rise again, to which of them will the woman belong? Because she has been the wife of each of the seven!' Jesus said to them: 'You are in error, and surely the reason is this: you do not understand the Scriptures or the power of God. After rising from the dead, men and women do not marry; they are as angels in heaven. As for proof that the dead do rise, have you not read in the Book of Moses, the passage on the Burning Bush, how God said to him: "I am the God of Abraham, the God of Isaac, the God of Jacob"? He is God not of dead men but of living. You are wandering far astray.'

Then one of the scribes came forward. He had been listening to the dispute and recognized that Jesus had answered well. So he asked him: 'Which is the first commandment of all?' Jesus answered: 'The first is: "Hear, O Israel, the Lord our God is one Lord, and you shall love the Lord your God with your whole heart, and with your whole soul, and with your whole mind, and with your whole strength." The second is: "You shall love your neighbour as yourself." There is no other commandment greater than these.' The scribe said to him: 'Admirable, Master! You have spoken truly, for God is one and there is no other but he, and to love him with your whole heart, and with your whole understanding, and with your whole strength, and to love your neigbour as yourself is something far greater than all holocausts and sacrifices.' Jesus acknowledged that he had spoken wisely by saying to him: 'You are not far from the kingdom of God.'

After this, no one ventured to put any more questions to him. Later, while teaching in the temple, Jesus himself put a question: 'How can the scribes say that the Messiah is David's son? David himself was moved by the Holy Spirit to say: "The Lord said to my Lord, sit at my right hand, until I make your enemies your footstool." David himself calls him "Lord"; how then can he be David's son?' *(Mk 12:13-37)*

Reflection

St Paul taught that the law of Moses is no longer binding on believers in Christ: 'Christ is the end of the law for those who believe,' he says in Romans (10:4). His doctrine was misunderstood and misrepresented. He was accused of teaching that the Christian is free from *all* law, and free to do as he likes. It cannot be denied that he exposed himself to this charge by some of the things he said. For example, he said: 'You are not under law but under grace' (Rom 6:14) — as if those who have the grace of the gospel have no law to obey of any kind. Some low-minded people appear to have drawn the extreme conclusion that actions formerly forbidden by the law of Moses, including gross sins against chastity, were no longer sins at all for Christians. St Paul therefore found it necessary to keep on repudiating this misinterpretation. That is what he is doing here.

At the beginning of the passage, the Greek is ambiguous. It can mean either: 'Join with me in imitating Christ', or 'Join together in imitating me.' Probably St Paul means both: when he was at Philippi, he acted in a Christlike way, so as to set a standard. Therefore, if the Philippians will imitate Paul, they will be imitating Christ. [1] But they must *not* imitate those whom he calls 'enemies of the cross of Christ' — men who have no desire to take up the cross, but on the contrary make a god of their belly and glory in their shame, men whose thoughts are pinned down to material things on the earth, and who regard their bodies as instruments of pleasure.

That way is not for us, St Paul says; *we* keep our thoughts raised upwards towards heaven, where Christ sits at the right hand of the Father. One day, he will come with power to destroy the forces of death and sin and weakness, and will transfigure these now humble bodies of ours into the likeness of his own glorious body. Meanwhile, we must live in this hope, reverencing our bodies — which are not *our* bodies — they belong not to us but to him; they are his instruments for good rather

---

[1] It is just possible that in Paul's private thoughts, 4:1 means that they will also imitate St Stephen. The word 'crown' in Greek is *stephanos,* and 'Stephen' is *Stephanos*. Is St Paul perhaps thinking that Stephen lives again in them, when they stand firm and look to heaven for Christ their Saviour? Cf. Acts 7:51—8:1, above, pp. 39-40, and Mk 6:16.

than our instruments of pleasure. We must keep them pure and undefiled for the day when he will come to take full possession of them and raise them to an intensity of life beyond anything we know, by transforming grace into glory. The excitement of human love at its purest is only a fleeting image of that pure incandescent life and love and peace in which the blessed share.

What St Paul is doing in the Epistle, Christ too is doing in the four disputes in the temple. He is instructing men whose minds are fastened down to the earth: men who are concerned about paying back to Caesar the coin on which Caesar has stamped his image, but have no thought of paying back to God their own bodies on which God has stamped his image; men who are so fascinated with the pleasures of marriage that they cannot imagine a heaven without sexual relations; men whose religious observance still consists in making fires, killing animals, pouring out blood, roasting meat, and eating it. In the last of the four incidents, Jesus himself takes the initiative and tries to raise up their thoughts above the narrow horizon of the temple by putting to them the enigmatic question about David's son. He does not supply the answer, but leaves them to think about the mysterious figure seated at God's right hand, waiting, until the day when his enemies will be crushed. God's universe may be much more mysterious than they have ever dared to imagine.

St Paul had two citizenships: he was a Roman citizen by birth, and a citizen of the heavenly Jerusalem by rebirth in baptism. He owed allegiance to the emperor in Rome, and to Christ reigning in heaven. At the time when he founded the church at Philippi, he had never seen Rome or the emperor; but he had seen Christ. His heavenly citizenship was quite as real to him as his Roman citizenship. Perhaps he wished to insinuate that the Philippians set too much store by their Roman citizenship. If he felt that the lesson of Christ's self-emptying was specially needed by the Christians of Philippi, perhaps the reason was that he saw in their close attachment to the emperor, as citizens of a Roman colony, an obstacle to their complete attachment to Christ their Saviour. Their special relationship to the emperor was the basis of their pride and self-assurance. St Paul seems to be saying: 'You must forget your former pride and joy as I did; you have two citizenships and two emperor-saviours, one in Rome and the other in the heavenly Jerusalem. Henceforth you must look to Christ.[1]

We too, in our day, have a double citizenship, one earthly and the other heavenly. How real to us is the latter? May God release our minds from the fascination of earthly things, and inspire us to keep our bodies holy, after the example of Christ our Lord and St Paul and all the heavenly court, especially our Lady, the Queen of heaven.

Prayer

Father almighty, who created us in your own image and likeness, detach our hearts from earthly things, and purify us daily through the Spirit of your Son, who lives and reigns with thee in the unity of the same Holy Spirit, and is God, for ever and ever.

---

[1] 3:15b probably means that if any of the Philippians have not yet learned to discount their social advantages, God will reveal this to them too, in time.

23
Jesus our Saviour

The Title 'Saviour'

As for us, our citizenship is in heaven. It is to heaven that we look expectantly for the Coming of Jesus Christ as our Saviour. He will transform our bodies from their present humble state into the likeness of the body which he has in his glory. For he has power to make all things subject to himself. So then, my dear and much loved brethren, my joy and my crown, persevere as you are in the Lord, my beloved. *(Phil 3:20—4:1)*

The Name 'Jesus'

An angel of the Lord appeared to Joseph in a dream, and said: 'Joseph, son of David, do not hesitate to take Mary to be your wife; for the child conceived by her is of the Holy Spirit. She will give birth to a son, and you shall call him Jesus, for it is he who will save his people from their sins.' *(Mt 1:20-21)*

Reflection

During the public ministry, when the disciples spoke to one another about Jesus, they did not refer to him as 'Jesus'. It would have sounded too familiar and therefore disrespectful. They called him 'Maran' or 'Rabban' — 'our Lord' or 'our Master', and Jesus approved of this. He said at the Last Supper, in connection with the Washing of Feet: 'You call me "Master" and "Lord", and rightly so, for that is what I am.'

This custom was maintained in the early Church. St Paul in his Epistles never speaks simply of 'Jesus'. In his main Epistle, he always speaks of 'our Lord Jesus Christ' or 'Christ Jesus our Lord' or the like. Only in the later Epistles (the Pastorals and 2 Peter), do we find that the title 'Saviour' is becoming common. The comparative rarity of this title in the rest of the New Testament is surprising, because the name 'Jesus' means 'Saviour', and the title 'Saviour' expresses more completely than 'Lord' the relationship of Christ to ourselves.

He is our Saviour in three senses: he is the one who saved us in the past, by his death on the cross; he is the one who now saves us through his forgiveness and enabling grace in the sacraments and in response to our prayers; and he is the one who will save us at the Last Day, as St Paul says in this passage of Philippians, by redeeming our bodies from death and corruption to life and glory.

To appreciate better our relationship to Christ our Saviour, each of us can compare himself to the man who went down from Jerusalem to Jericho and fell among thieves. They left him 'half-dead', which means, I suppose, unconscious. When he regained consciousness on the following day, his saviour or saver, the Good Samaritan, was gone; but the innkeeper was able to tell him the name of his saviour, that his saviour had paid the cost of his cure and convalescence, and that he had promised to return. That is a picture of our condition. We wake up to find ourselves in the Church, and the innkeeper who looks after us tells us the name of our Saviour, tells us that the expenses of our cure have been paid by our Saviour, and tells us that one day he will return.[1] Christ saved us in the past, at great cost to himself; he keeps us safe now within the Church; and one day he will come as Saviour to glorify our frail and humble bodies. Therefore Christ is behind us, in the past; Christ is above us, in the present; and Christ is before us, in the future, at the Judgment. We live surrounded by his unseen presence and beneficent care. As a Hebrew would say, we live in his Name.

Prayer

Lord Jesus, our Saviour, be with us in this life to preserve us from sin; keep us faithful to your teaching, so that when you come to judge the world, we may be found worthy of admission to your kingdom.

---

[1] The innkeeper also tells us that the four gospels give us a reliable account of what our Saviour said and did. Gratitude should dispose us to accept this account.

24
The Book of Life

Friction at Philippi

So then, my dear and much loved brethren, my joy and my crown, persevere as you are in the Lord, my beloved. I beg of you, Evodia, and I beg of you, Syntyche, to agree with each other in the Lord. And I would ask you, my faithful comrade, to help these women, who shared my labours for the gospel — as also did Clement and my other helpers. Their names are written in the Book of Life. *(Phil 4:1-3)*

Treasure in Heaven

He who does not take his cross and follow me is not worthy of me. He who finds his life will lose it, and he who loses his life for my sake will find it.

He who welcomes you, welcomes me; and he who welcomes me, welcomes him who sent me. He who welcomes a prophet because he is a prophet, will receive a prophet's reward; and he who welcomes a just man because he is a just man, will receive a just man's reward. And whoever gives one of these little ones a cup of cold water because he is a disciple, I tell you truly, he will not go unrewarded. (*Mt 10:38-42*)

Reflection

St Paul is one who lost his life in order to find it. In this section of the Epistle, he rejoices to think that the Philippians have followed his example. They are his joy and his crown, so long as they persevere in the Christlike way of life which he taught them.

But he is a little saddened by the strained relationship between two of his former helpers, Evodia and Syntyche, who shared his trials when he first preached in Greece and helped him with their means (cf. 4: 14-15). On the strength of Jesus' word about the cup of cold water, St Paul can say confidently that their names are written in the Book of Life — they will not go unrewarded. In spite of their present alienation from each other, they will be reunited in God's kingdom. Their past merits will not be forgotten. As the Epistle to the Hebrews puts it, 'God is not unjust, that he should forget' (6: 10). When recent lapses are forgiven, old merits are revived.

St Paul is careful not to take sides in the dispute. He avoids saying 'I call upon Evodia and Syntyche', for fear Syntyche might say: 'Why did he put Evodia before me?' To preserve impartiality as far as is possible, he repeats the verb: 'I call upon you, Evodia, and I call upon you, Syntyche.' He is pulled in two directions again, and does not know which to choose. Se he appeals to an unnamed 'yoke-fellow' to help them to achieve reconciliation quickly. This will not be difficult if they will heed the main lesson of the Epistle, that unity is to be preserved by humility, self-emptying, and willingness to take the lower place. They are repeating the mistake of the sons of Zebedee (Mt 20-21) and of the Pharisees whom Jesus saw vying for the first places at a banquet (Lk 14:7). If each of them would listen to Paul's advice to be humble and regard others as better than herself (2:3), such tension would never occur.

It is sad to see how often the peace of a parish or religious community is upset by rivalry and jealousy over who should do what. Those who are eager to play their part in the apostolic work of the Church are worthy of praise — provided they do not wish to exclude others or to put them in their place (cf. 1:17).

Prayer

Deliver us, O Lord, from the evil of jealousy. Let us live at peace with all men, especially our kindred in the faith, whose names are written in heaven. May your peace reign on earth, as it does in heaven.

25
Joy and Peace

Christian Courtesy

Rejoice in the Lord at all times. I will say it again: Rejoice! Let your gentleness be known to all men. The Lord is near. Do not give way to anxiety; in every need let your requests be known to God, in prayer and petition, joined with thanksgiving. Then God's peace, which passes all understanding, will keep watch over your hearts and thoughts in Christ Jesus. For the rest, brethren, devote your minds to all that is true, and venerable, and just, and holy, and lovable, and seemly, and good, and praiseworthy. Imitate in your conduct what you have observed, and learned, and heard, and seen, in me; and God, the author of peace will be with you. *(Phil 4:4-9)*

Heathen Cares

Do not be anxious about what you eat or drink for the support of your life, nor about what clothes you wear for the good of your body. Is not your life something greater than its food, and your body something greater than its clothing? Look at the birds of the air: they do not sow, or reap, or gather into barns, yet your heavenly Father looks after them. Are you not much more valuable than they are? And which of you, by setting his mind to it, could add eighteen inches to his height? Why are you anxious about your clothes? Look at the lillies of the field and how they grow: they do not labour, they do not spin, and yet I tell you, not even Solomon in all his glory was dressed as splendidly as one of these. If then God clothes in this way the grass of the field, which lives today and tomorrow is thrown into the oven, will he not do even more for you, men of little faith? Then do not ask, What are we going to eat? or, What are we going to drink? or, What are we going to wear? Those are the things the heathen are bent upon. Do not give way to anxiety, for your heavenly Father is aware that you need all these things. Seek first the kingdom of God and his justice; then all those things will be given to you in addition. *(Mt 6:25-33)*

Reflection

Having exhorted Evodia and Syntyche to be charitable to each other, St Paul goes on to speak of joy and peace. Remembering that all their names are written in heaven, the Philippians ought to rejoice in the Lord (cf. Lk 10:20). If they do, they will be cheerful people, who will command the attention and admiration of all men by their *epieikeia*, that is, by their gentleness, modesty and courtesy.

The secret of preserving such an agreeable exterior lies within. Christian courtesy springs from a life of faith and prayer. Following the example of Jesus in the Sermon on the Mount, St Paul warns us against anxiety, which of its nature drives out joy and disturbs peace. When

Jesus first spoke his warning against anxiety, he was probably talking about prayer — saying: 'When you turn to prayer, put out of your mind all material worries; trust God our Father to look after them; do not come to prayer with a shopping list; seek first, in prayer, the kingdom of God and his justice. Then your heavenly Father will supply all your wants.'

In the same way, St Paul says: 'Do not worry! Do not give way to anxiety, but make known your needs to God in prayer, thanking him for all his goodness, and trusting him to take care of your needs. Then the peace of God which passes all understanding will keep guard over your hearts, and over your thoughts.' Those who are in the habit of speaking to God in prayer and casting all their cares upon him, do not find it hard to put away all vulgar and trivial thoughts, worldly and fleshly thoughts, bitter, complaining and ungrateful thoughts. Such people will think only of what is true and venerable and just and holy and lovable and seemly and good and praiseworthy; their inner peace, sobriety and dignity will flow out into their external conduct, and their gentleness and courtesy will be known to all men. Notice the connection: 'If your needs are known to God, your kindness will be known to all men.' St Paul is speaking from immediate experience here: he refuses to worry over his imprisonment and poverty, because he believes that God knows best and God will provide. As a result, he enjoys a peace which passes his understanding, and his cheerful courage commends the gospel to all in the garrison.

The fruits of the Spirit are charity, joy and peace. They belong to those whose thoughts are not bent down to the earth like the eyes of an animal, but raised upwards to the heavenly Jerusalem, the city of peace, where Christ lives and reigns at the right hand of the Father. Here is a practical test of the Christian quality of our thoughts: they should always be such that if someone says suddenly: 'A penny for your thoughts!' we can always reply, simply and without a blush: 'I was thinking of this' or 'I was thinking of that' — something true, venerable, just, holy, lovable, seemly and good.

Courtesy, gentleness and modesty — this was the impression which Jesus himself left with his disciples, as can be seen from a passage of the Epistle to Titus (2: 11-14) which strongly resembles the present section of Philippians: 'The grace of God has been revealed, bringing salvation to all mankind, teaching us to renounce ungodliness and worldly desires, and to live temperate, just and holy lives in this present world, while we look forward to our blessed hope, the revelation of the glory of our great God and Saviour, Jesus Christ, who offered himself for us, to ransom us from all wickedness, to cleanse us, and to make us his own people, zealous to do good.'

Prayer

Heavenly Father, from whom all good things descend, we entrust to you all our needs of soul and body, asking only that you will fill our hearts with gratitude and with that peace which passes all understanding. Send your Holy Spirit upon us, so that we may pray as we ought and walk before you in justice.

26

Apostolic Poverty

An Embarrassing Gift

It gave me great joy in the Lord to see that after all this time your thoughtfulness for me had borne fruit once more — of course you had been thoughtful all the time, but you had no opportunity to show it. I do not mean that I was in real need. I have learned to content myself with whatever I have. I know how to be abased, and I know how to abound. I am already fully initiated in everything, in being satisfied and going hungry, in enjoying plenty and going short. I can manage either way, through him who gives me strength. However, it was kind of you to send me assistance in my affliction. You will remember, men of Philippi, that in the early days of the gospel, when I left Macedonia, with no other church did I have an exchange of help, but you alone sent assistance to me, at Thessalonica, on two occasions, to meet my needs. I am eager not so much for the gift, but rather for the spiritual profit that accrues to your account. I have all that I need and more. I am fully provided for, now that I have received from Epaphroditus what you sent — a fragrant sacrifice, an acceptable offering, pleasing to God. My God will supply your every need

from his treasury of glory in Christ Jesus. To God who is our Father be glory for ever and ever. Amen.
(*Phil 4:10-20*)

The Safeguards of Sincerity

Jesus said to the twelve: 'Go and proclaim that the kingdom of heaven is near. Cure the sick, raise the dead, cleanse lepers, drive out devils. What you have received as a gift, give as a gift. Get no gold or silver or copper for your purse; no knapsack for the journey; no second coat; no sandals or staff. For the labourer has a right to his keep. When you go into a city or village, inquire after a worthy household, and lodge there until you leave.

He who welcomes you, welcomes me; and he who welcomes me, welcomes him who sent me. He who welcomes a prophet because he is a prophet will receive a prophet's reward; and he who welcomes a just man because he is a just man will receive a just man's reward.
(*Mt 10:7-10, 40-41*)

Reflection

In this closing section of the Epistle, it transpires that St Paul is writing to thank the Philippians for a gift of money. There were veiled allusions to this gift at the very beginning, when he expressed his joy over the share the Philippians had taken in spreading the gospel from the earliest days to the present. But he does not actually come to the point and say 'Thank you' until right at the end. And when he does at last come to the point here, he does not speak with the simplicity and humility we might have expected. On the contrary, the passage is embarrassed, confused, and at one point almost discourteous. Just imagine if someone had saved up and sent you a gift, and you wrote back saying: 'What I value is not the gift, but the spiritual profit you have gained by this sacrifice'!

Some learned critics have thought that Paul, being a man of good social standing, found it distasteful to speak about money, was embarrassed at receiving it, and still had so much of the Pharisee left in him that he was unable to conceal his embarrassment. But there is a kinder explanation, which is more likely to be the true one.

When St Paul went up to Jerusalem from the Apostolic Council described in Acts 15 and Galatians 2, Peter, James and John asked him to collect alms in the Gentile churches for the poor of Jerusalem, and he undertook to do so. He went off and organized the collection among the Galatians, Macedonians and Corinthians, on a basis of weekly subscriptions. The sums of money collected must have been quite large, and they were sent off to Jerusalem. What happened to them, we have no idea; and perhaps the Galatians, Macedonians and Corithians had no idea either. At all events, some of them began to suspect Paul's motives and to accuse him of rapacity. They said he was making money out of preaching the gospel.

He knew that people would not accept the gospel if they suspected his motives in preaching it. That was the reasoning behind our Lord's rules for missionaries working among the unconverted: they might accept their daily bread, because the labourer is worthy of his keep; but they were not to receive gifts and fill their wallets with gold and silver, or to buy themselves superfluous clothes; nor were they to move up the social ladder from one house to another; they were to find a worthy household, even if a poor one, and stay there till they left the place; and when they left, they were to be no richer than when they arrived. In this way they would demonstrate the purity of their motives. Those were Christ's instructions to the apostles. But on the other hand, he promised a rich reward to those who gave food and drink and lodging to his apostles: they would receive the reward of an apostle.

So what is St Paul to say when he receives this gift of money? He does not absolutely need it. The people of Caesar's household would not let him starve. And he does not want to appear too grateful, or he may seem to be asking for further gifts. On the other hand, he is glad to have the money, and he is glad to know that the Philippians will receive the rich reward promised by our Lord to such generous people. So the gift did place him in a delicate position — he *is* embarrassed, though not out of pride — and what he says shows a good deal of prudence, even of tact. He probably foresaw that the letter would circulate through the other churches of Macedonia; and therefore he discreetly let it be known, to all whom it might concern, that he had received money only three times from Philippi, and from no other Macedonian church. No one could say that he was doing well out of the gospel.

From these reflections we can draw two lessons, one for the laity and one for the clergy. The laity must remember Christ's promise and be generous in assisting the Church in her missionary and charitable enterprises. The clergy must remember his prohibitions and avoid all self-seeking and all appearance of self-seeking. The practice of poverty is a guarantee of apostolic sincerity. If people suspect a preacher's motives, they will not heed his message.

Prayer

Grant, O Lord, that all who teach the Christian faith may have a pure intention, so that their hearers will see their sincerity, believe their message, and give glory to you, our Father in heaven.

27
Reunion of the Human Family

Gentiles consecrated to God

Greetings to everyone who has been made holy in Christ Jesus. The brethren who are with me greet you. All who are holy greet you, especially those of Caesar's household. The grace of the Lord Jesus Christ be with your spirit.
(Phil 4:21-23)

The Voice of Truth

I am the Good Shepherd. I know my own and my own know me, just as the Father knows me and I know the Father; and I will lay down my life for the sheep. I have other sheep too, not of this fold. Those too I must lead; they will heed my voice, and there will be one flock and one Shepherd. *(Jn 10:14-16)*

Reflection

In the parable from St John, the sheepfold is Israel, and the other sheep are non-Israelites, i.e., Gentiles, who will respond to the preaching of the gospel. Jesus expresses the same idea again, without the pastoral imagery, when speaking to the Gentile governor, Pilate: 'For this I was born and came into the world: to bear witness to the truth; everyone who is of the truth hears my voice.' In these words we hear the Good Shepherd appealing to one of his Gentile sheep. Pilate did not at once respond, but according to many Christian legends he did later. The final greeting of the Epistle shows that St Paul too made his appeal to members of the household of Caesar — and found a hearing. In the preaching of Paul they heard the voice of Christ. Paul understood the mind of Christ, and followed in his footsteps, and spoke as his ambassador.

The words of Jesus to the Syro-Phoenician woman in the synoptic gospels has a very different sound, more congenial, no doubt, to the judaizing teachers than to Paul. This Gentile woman comes to Christ and pleads for the cure of her daughter (Mt 15:21-28). He seems to treat her very badly. At first he ignores her. Then his disciples intervene, and he says: 'I am sent only to the lost sheep of the house of Israel.' And when the woman persists, he says: 'It is not right to take the children's bread and throw it to dogs.' Harsh words!

During his public ministry, the work of Jesus was restricted to Israel, and he imposed the same restriction on his disciples (Mt 10:5): 'Go nowhere among the Gentiles, and enter no town of the Samaritans.' But he removed this restriction after his resurrection, when he met his disciples on a mountain in Galilee of the Gentiles and sent them to teach all nations (Mt 28:19). The gospel is a unifying force. It aims to unite all men, of all nations, in one flock under the one Shepherd, Christ, the new Adam. This is the gospel of reconciliation which St Paul was sent to preach to the Gentiles.

There is no chosen people enjoying a monopoly of God's love and favour. Every soul is precious in God's eyes: we are created one by one, justified and made 'holy' through his sacraments one by one, and judged one by one. Every individual of every nation is important to God, and therefore has infinite value. This conception, of the infinite value of the individual, was ultimately fatal to slavery. If it took centuries to produce its effect, the reason is in part that all men cherish illusions of superiority and cling to privilege. But perhaps St Paul too retarded the effect of his own preaching by his great insistence on submission to the powers that be (Rom 13:1), a principle which tends to eternalize the status quo. His theology was radical enough, but in his social thinking he was a conservative. It took the Church a very long time to carry out the needed adjustment.

The same principle of the infinite value of *every* human individual made the Nazis hostile to Christianity. They could not stomach it, and tried in vain to stamp it out.

The same principle is much needed in the world today. If men of different nations and races are going to live together, work together, and play together in peace and charity, they must begin by holding one another in respect as made in God's image and precious in his sight. That is the only basis for the universal love which is commanded in the Sermon on the Mount: we must imitate the all-embracing love of God our Father, who sends his sun and his rain for all of us alike, and who gave his only Son that whosoever believes in him, of whatever race, may not perish but may have eternal life.

Prayer

Come, Lord Jesus, and extend your dominion over all mankind, wise and foolish, slave and free, black and white. Join us all as brothers in reverence to God our Father.

Appendix 1

THE PLACE AND DATE OF COMPOSITION OF PHILIPPIANS

St Paul founded the church of Philippi in A.D. 49, during his second missionary journey (cf. Acts 16:11-40). The Epistle to the Philippians, written some years later (cf. 4:15), is one of the 'Captivity Epistles', i.e. at the time of writing St Paul was in prison (cf. 1:14).

After his one-night detention in prison at Philippi itself (Acts 16:23-46), the Acts of the Apostles mentions only two other periods of imprisonment: two years at Caesarea in A.D. 58-60 (Acts 24:7) and two years at Rome in A.D. 61-63 (Acts 28:16). Until fairly recently, commentators have usually held that Philippians was written during the Roman captivity of A.D. 61-63. There are, however, serious difficulties in this view: (1) The Epistle shows that from his prison St Paul maintained close contact with Philippi; messengers were coming and going frequently. Communications between Rome and the colony at the end of the Via Egnatia were good, but even so the journey must have taken about a month.[1]

---

[1] Philippi in Macedonia was the scene of the victory of Antony and Octavian (later Augustus) over Brutus and

This suggests that St Paul's prison was somewhere closer to Philippi. (2) The last paragraph of the Epistle shows that the gift sent from Philippi to Paul in prison was the first contribution which he had received since his stay in Thessalonica during the second missionary journey. Yet between this date and his arrival in Rome he visited them on two further occasions (cf. 2 Cor 1:15), when they would have had an opportunity to help him (cf. Phil 4:10). (3) If the Epistles to the Colossians and to Philemon were written during the Roman captivity, there is the problem of explaining the difference in style between Philippians and these Epistles.

In view of these difficulties, many scholars now hold that Philippians was written during an earlier imprisonment which is not recorded in the Acts of the Apostles. The Second Epistle to the Corinthians, written in A.D. 57, shows that at that date St Paul had already been imprisoned a number of times (cf. 2 Cor 6:5; 11:23). It has been conjectured that at least one of these imprisonments took place during his long stay in Ephesus (cf. Acts 19:10); and this may have been the occasion when he almost despaired of his life (cf. 2 Cor 1:8).

If the Epistle to the Philippians was written during this imprisonment (say in A.D. 56), the comings and goings between the prison and Philippi are more easily understandable. It is also easier to see why the Philippians had no opportunity to furnish St Paul with financial help. The movements of Timothy and Paul projected in Phil 2:19-24 agree well with the description of the end of St Paul's stay at Ephesus in Acts 19:21-22 and 20:21. On the whole, Ephesus seems more likely than Rome as the place from which St Paul wrote to the Philippians.

Cassius in 42 B.C. Veterans of the victorious legions were settled there, and the city was given the high status of a 'colony'.

Appendix 2

THE TEXT OF THE EPISTLE

1 Paul and Timothy, servants of Christ Jesus, to all who have been made holy in Christ Jesus at Philippi, and to your bishops and deacons: ² grace to you and peace from God our Father and from the Lord Jesus Christ. ³ I give thanks to my God for all your remembrance of me, ⁴ always in all my prayers for you all, offering my prayers with joy ⁵ over the share you have taken in spreading the gospel, from the earliest days to the present time. ⁶ And I am confident that he who began this good work in you will continue to complete it until the Day of Christ Jesus. ⁷ It is but right for me to think of you all in this way, because you ever hold me in your hearts, when I am in prison, when I am on trial, when I am defending the gospel — you who are all sharers in the privilege granted to me. ⁸ And God is my witness, how I long for you all in the heart of Christ Jesus. ⁹ This too is my prayer: that your love may abound more and more in all knowledge and discernment, ¹⁰ so that you may always recognize what is best, and thus arrive faultless and blameless at the Lord's Assize, ¹¹ laden with the fruits of justice produced in you through Jesus Christ, for the glory and praise of God.

¹² I should like you to know, brethren, that my situation here has turned out to be more of a help than a hindrance to the progress of the gospel. ¹³ Everyone in the fortress, and outside as well, has come to know that I am imprisoned for Christ's sake. ¹⁴ And most of our brethren in the Lord have been encouraged by my imprisonment to show even greater boldness in preaching the word of God. ¹⁵ Some preach through envy and ambition, others with a good will. ¹⁶ Those

who proclaim Christ out of love, do so because they know that I am confined here for the defence of the gospel; [17] the others, not for any holy motive, but out of rivalry — they think to cause me further affliction in my imprisonment. [18] But why should I mind, so long as one way or another, whether sincerely or for less worthy motives, Christ is being preached. Meanwhile, I am in good spirits and shall continue to be so.

[19] I am confident that this whole affair will end with my liberation, through your prayers and through an abundant outpouring of the Spirit of Jesus Christ. [20] For it is my hope and expectation that far from being put to shame, I shall speak out confidently, so that Christ will be glorified, now as always, in my person — whether I am to live, or whether I am to die. [21] For, so far as I am concerned, to live is Christ, and to die will be a gain. [22] But if to live on in the flesh means that I shall do fruitful work — then I do not know what to choose, [23] I am pulled in two directions, longing to depart this life and be with Christ (which is far the better thing); [24] and yet, for your sake, it is more expedient that I should remain in the flesh. [25] Therefore I am confident that I shall stay and stand by you all, to sustain your progress and your joy in the faith. [26] Then you will have even greater confidence in Christ Jesus on my account, when I return to be with you.

[27] Be sure that the life of your community is worthy of the gospel, so that whether I come and see you or receive news of you at a distance, I may know that you are standing firm, united in spirit, battling with one soul through faith in the gospel, [28] and refusing to be in any way put out by your enemies. To them your constancy is a warning of their doom, granted by God; to you it is a pledge of your salvation: [29] you have been allowed to take Christ's side, not only by believing in him, but also by suffering for him, [30] sharing the same trials which you once saw me undergo and now hear that I am undergoing again.

2 [1] So then, if a word of encouragement in Christ, if an appeal made in love, if fellowship in the Spirit, if tenderness and compassion have any power with you, [2] bring my joy to completion, by being all of one mind, united in one love, living by one soul, sharing one mind. [3] Do nothing from jealousy or empty ambition; be humble; believe, each of you, that the others are better than you are; [4] look to your neighbour's interest rather than to your own. [5] Let there be one mind in you, the mind of Christ, [6] who, being in the form of God, did not make it his ambition to be treated as God, [7] but emptied himself, and took the form of a servant. He was born in the manner of men, and wearing the appearance of man, [8] he humbled himself, and was obedient unto death, even to death on a cross. [9] Therefore God exalted him greatly, and bestowed on him the name that is above all names, [10] so that in the name of Jesus every knee shall bend, in heaven, on earth, and under the earth, [11] and every tongue acclaim Jesus Christ as 'Lord', to the glory of God his Father.

[12] So then, my dear friends, just as you have always been obedient in my presence, so now still more in my absence: continue in fear and trembling to work out your salvation. [13] For God is present, working among you, enabling you both to will and to accomplish his good pleasure. [14] Continue without grumbling or disputes. [15] In this way you will be faultless and without defect, innocent children of God, in the midst of a crooked and perverse generation. Shine out before them as beacons in the world, [16] offering the word of life. Then I shall be able to boast, on the Day of Christ's Judgment, that I did not run my course in vain, I did not labour for nothing. [17] Although my life is being poured out as a libation upon the sacrificial offering of your faith, yet I rejoice for my own sake and for yours; [18] and you too must rejoice both for your own sake and for mine as well.

[19] I hope in the Lord Jesus that I shall be sending Timothy to you soon, so that I may receive some cheering news of how things are with you. [20] I have no one who understands me as he does, and no one who will show such true concern for your well-being. [21] All the rest work for their own interests, not for Christ. [22] But Timothy has proved his worth, as you know; he has worked beside me in the service of the gospel like a son working with his father. [23] So I am hoping to send him to you without further delay, as soon as I can foresee the outcome of my case; [24] and I am confident that I shall be coming myself before long.

[25] Meanwhile, I think it advisable to send back to you Epaphroditus, my brother, the sharer of my labours and battles, and your messenger, sent to minister to my needs. [26] He has been homesick for you all and upset because you had heard that he was ill. [27] He was indeed ill, and nearly died; but God had mercy on him — and not on him alone, but on me as well, or there would have been a fresh grief added to my

others. ²⁸ So I am sending him to you sooner than I would have done, so that you will have the joy of seeing him again, and I shall be free of anxiety. ²⁹ Give him a truly joyful and Christian welcome. You must hold in honour a man like this, ³⁰ who came near to death in Christ's service, and risked his life to do for me the one remaining thing which you had not been able to do in my service.

3 ¹ For the rest, my brethren, rejoice in the Lord. To keep repeating the same advice 'causes me no apprehension, and to you no peril brings'. ² Beware of dogs, beware of malefactors, beware of mutilation of the flesh. ³ It is we who are the true circumcision — we who worship in the Spirit of God, who place our trust in Christ Jesus, and put no confidence in the flesh. ⁴ And yet I have grounds for confidence in the flesh — indeed if anyone has I have still more: ⁵ circumcised on my eighth day, an Israelite by birth, of the tribe of Benjamin, Hebrew-speaking and of Hebrew-speaking parents; in regard to the law a Pharisee; ⁶ as for my zeal, I persecuted the Church; as for the justice that comes from the law, there was nothing wrong with me. ⁷ But all those things that were to my credit, for Christ's sake I now consider liabilities. ⁸ In fact there is now nothing I do not regard as such, so far does the privilege of knowing Christ Jesus my Lord surpass all other advantages. For his sake I have forfeited all those things, I count them as a refuse, in order to win Christ, ⁹ to be in him, and to possess not a justice of my own making, based on the law, but the justice that comes through faith in Christ, God's justice, based on faith, ¹⁰ so that I may know him and experience the power of his resurrection and fellowship in his sufferings. I become like him in his death, ¹¹ in the hope of attaining the resurrection from the dead.

¹² I do not say that I have already won the prize or reached perfection, but I am pressing on to take hold of it — or rather, Christ has taken hold of me. ¹³ Brethren, I do not consider myself to have won the prize already; but one thing I claim: I forget about what is behind and strain towards what is ahead, ¹⁴ and press on to the finishing line to win the prize of the high vocation to which God has called me in Christ Jesus. ¹⁵ So then, let us view our lives in this way, those of us who are perfect; if you take any other view, God will reveal the truth of this one to you in time. ¹⁶ Only let us persevere in the course we are now pursuing.

[17] Brethren, unite in following my example, and keep your eyes on those who live according to the model which my own conduct set before you. [18] There are many who go a far different way. I have often told you before, and now I tell you with tears: they are enemies of the cross of Christ, [19] and their end will be utter ruin. Their god is their belly; they glory in their shame; their hearts are bent on earthly things. [20] But as for us, our citizenship is in heaven; it is to heaven that we look expectantly for the Coming of Jesus Christ as our Saviour. [21] He will transform our bodies from their present humble state into the likeness of the body which he has in his glory, for he has the power to make all things subject to himself.

4 So then, my dear and much loved brethren, my joy and my crown, persevere as you are in the Lord, my beloved.

[2] I beg of you, Evodia, and I beg of you, Syntyche, to agree with each other in the Lord. [3] And I would ask you, [2]my faithful comrade, to help these women, who shared my labours for the gospel — as also did Clement and my other helpers. Their names are written in the Book of Life. [4] Rejoice in the Lord at all times. I will say it again: Rejoice! [5] Let your gentleness be known to all men. The Lord is near. [6] Do not give way to anxiety; in every need, let your request be known to God, in prayer and petition joined with thanksgiving. [7] Then God's peace, which passes all understanding, will keep watch over your hearts and thoughts in Christ Jesus. [8] For the rest, brethren, devote your minds to all that is true, and venerable, and just, and holy, and lovable, and seemly, and good, and praiseworthy. [9] Imitate in your conduct what you have observed, and learned, and heard, and seen, in me; and God, the author of peace, will be with you.

[10] It gave me great joy in the Lord to see that after all this time your thoughtfulness for me had borne fruit once more — of course you have been thoughtful all the time, but you had no opportunity to show it. [11] I do not mean that I was in real need. [12] I have learned to content myself with whatever I have. I know how to be abased, and I know how to abound. I am already initiated in everything — in being satisfied and going hungry, in enjoying plenty and going short. [13] I can manage either way, through him who gives me strength. [14] However, it was kind of you to send me assistance in my affliction. [15] You will remember, men of Philippi, that in the early days of the gospel, when I left Macedonia, with no other church did I have an exchange of help, [16] but you

alone sent assistance to me, at Thessalonica, on two occasions, to meet my needs. [17] I am eager not so much for the gift, but rather for the spiritual profit that accrues to your account. [18] I have all that I need and more. I am fully provided for, now that I have received from Epaphroditus what you sent — a fragrant sacrifice, an acceptable offering, pleasing to God. [19] My God will supply your every need from his treasury of glory in Christ Jesus.

[20] To God who is our Father be glory for ever and ever. [21] Greetings to everyone who has been made holy in Christ Jesus. [22] The brethren who are with me greet you, and so do all God's people here, especially those of Caesar's household. [23] The grace of the Lord Jesus Christ be with your spirit. Amen.

GOSPEL PASSAGES QUOTED

Matthew

1:20-21	The Name 'Jesus'	104
6:25-33	Seeking the Kingdom	110
8:1-13	Cure of a Leper, Centurion's Son	75
9:32-37	Jesus and the People	66
10:7-10, 40-41	Rules for Missionaries	114
10:38-42	Rewards for Hospitality	107
12:9-21	Curing on the Sabbath	23
19:16-22	The Rich Young Man	95
20:1-15	The Labourers in the Vineyard	14
20:20-28	Request of the Sons of Zebedee	43
23:1-12	Denunciation of Scribes and Pharisees	71
25:31-46	The Last Judgment	10
26:6-13	The Anointing at Bethany	58

Mark

3:32-35	The True Brethren of Jesus	19
8:34-38	Conditions of Discipleship	40
12:13-37	Disputes in the Temple	99
15:33-39	The Death of Christ	50

Luke

2:6-14	The Birth of Jesus	46
10:25-37	The Good Samaritan	79
12:16-20	The Rich Fool	31
23:32-33, 38-43	The Good Thief	86
26:36-47	Jesus appears to his Disciples	90

John

10:14-16	The Good Shepherd	119
12:1-5	The Anointing at Bethany	62
13:2-15	The Washing of Feet	54
13:30-32	The Departure of Judas	27
15:1-7	The True Vine	35

SCRIPTURE FOR MEDITATION

This series is designed to present the fruits of recent Scriptural research in a form useful for private meditation, liturgical preaching, and classroom teaching.

> 'We know of no other popular level series in which the riches and depth of Sacred Scripture are so inspiringly revealed. The reader is given every thrill of the explorer seeking the pearl of great price.' — *The Irish Catholic*.

Other books in this series:

1. THE INFANCY NARRATIVES, by John Bligh. The Infancy Narratives of St Luke and St Matthew are taken in consecutive sections. Each is compared with an appropriate passage from the Old Testament.
   Published in 1968 — 10s. 6d.

3. OUR DIVINE MASTER, by John Bligh. A compact synthesis of the teaching of Christ on personal relationships: God and man, ruler and subject, Jew and Gentile, rich and poor, man and wife, etc.
   Ready about Easter, 1969 — 10s. 6d.

4. COLOSSIANS, by John Bligh. Offers an original interpretation of St Paul's Epistle to the Colossians in the form of 'reflections' or homilies.
   Ready about September, 1969 — 10s. 6d.

St Paul Publications

Coming shortly:

A major Catholic commentary (570 pages):

GALATIANS, by John Bligh.

Besides offering a detailed exegesis of this key Epistle of St Paul, the commentary is an excellent introduction to Pauline theology. Knowledge of Greek is not presupposed.

Ready about Easter, 1969 — 84s. approx.

* * *

For readers who are proficient in Biblical Greek:

GALATIANS IN GREEK, by John Bligh.

Published by the University of Detroit, 1966 — $5
(in the U.K. 40s.)